● MORE PRAISE FOR *I'M A WILD SEED* ●

"Full of life and heart and light,
I'm a Wild Seed is as hilarious as it is heartbreaking,
offering a deeply empathetic graphic manual for our time."
—KRISTEN RADTKE, Author of *Imagine Wanting Only This*

●

"Love is love, live your most authentic life,
and let others live theirs is Sharon Lee De La Cruz's
underlying message. Her honest memoir thoughtfully deconstructs
and reconstructs gender, sexuality and race through
Cruz's own unique and personal life lens."
—TRACY WHITE, Author of *How I Made It to Eighteen*

●

"A sweet and spirited memoir about navigating,
understanding, and ultimately celebrating
the many facets of one's identity."
—WHIT TAYLOR, Author of *Ghost Stories*

SHARON LEE DE LA CRUZ

I'M A WILD SEED

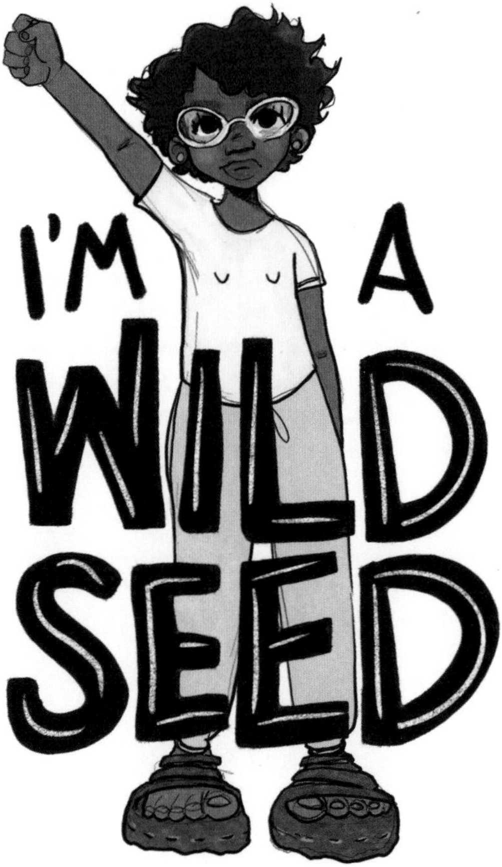

STREET NOISE

STREET NOISE BOOKS · BROOKLYN, NEW YORK

This book is dedicated to Marsha "pay it no mind" Johnson
and to our loved trans sisters who we have lost
in the fight for freedom.

●

ISBN 978-1951-491-05-5

Edited by Ellen Lindner
Book design by David DeWitt and Liz Frances

Printed in China

9 8 7 6 5 4 3 2 1

First Edition

be free
baby
colora,
be free

• Contents •

I think my neck is stuck in this position forever

If I stay like this forever, maybe I won't have to pay bills anymore

FART

INTRO

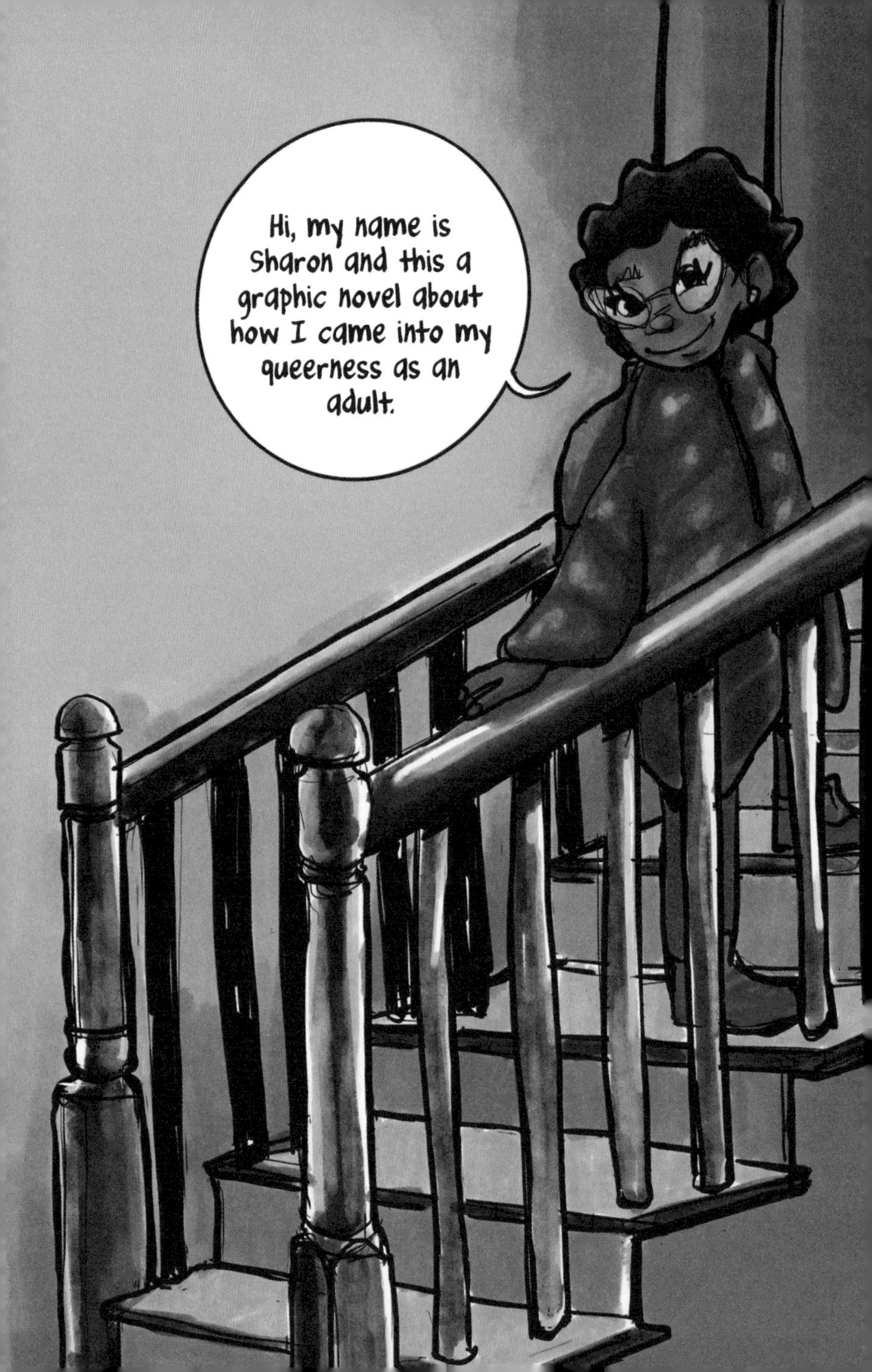
Hi, my name is Sharon and this a graphic novel about how I came into my queerness as an adult.

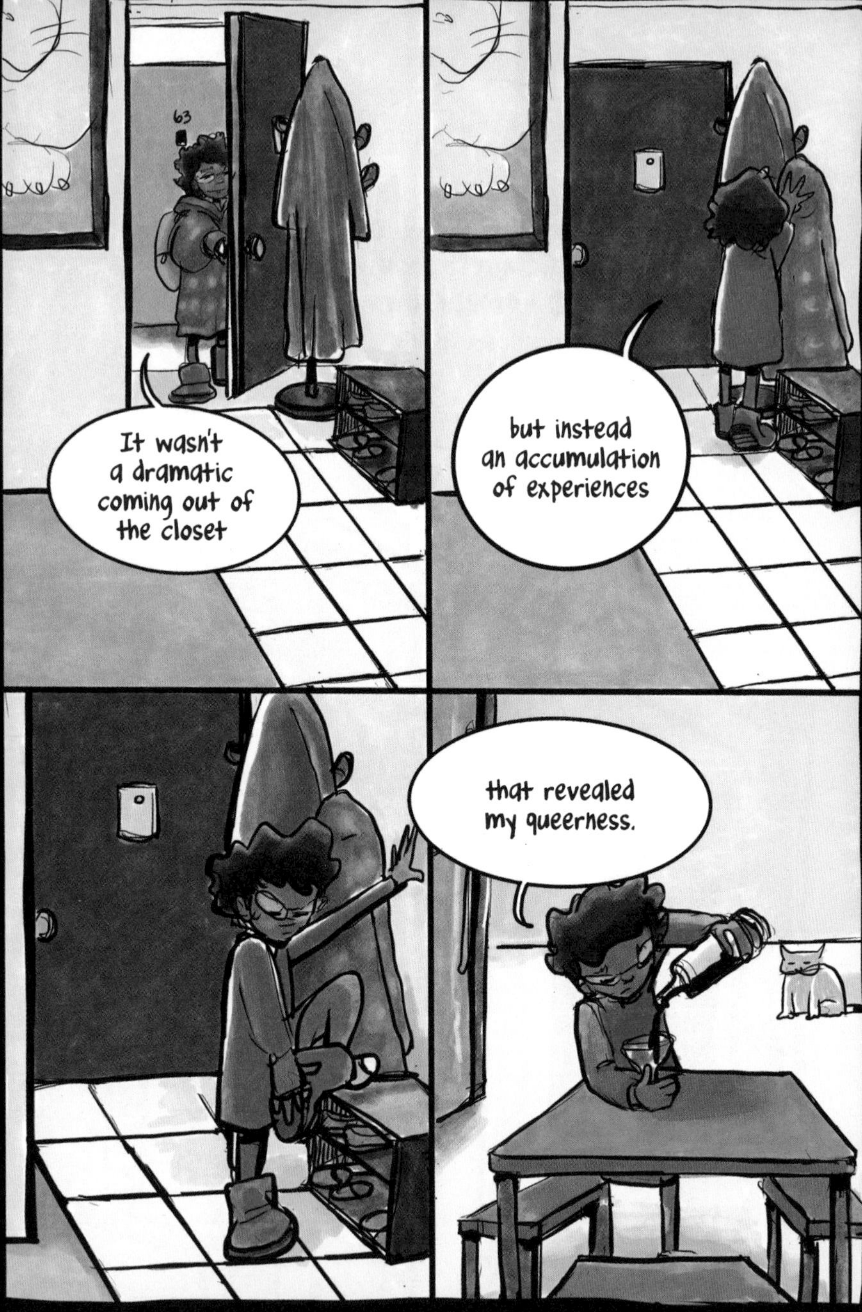
63
It wasn't a dramatic coming out of the closet
but instead an accumulation of experiences
that revealed my queerness.

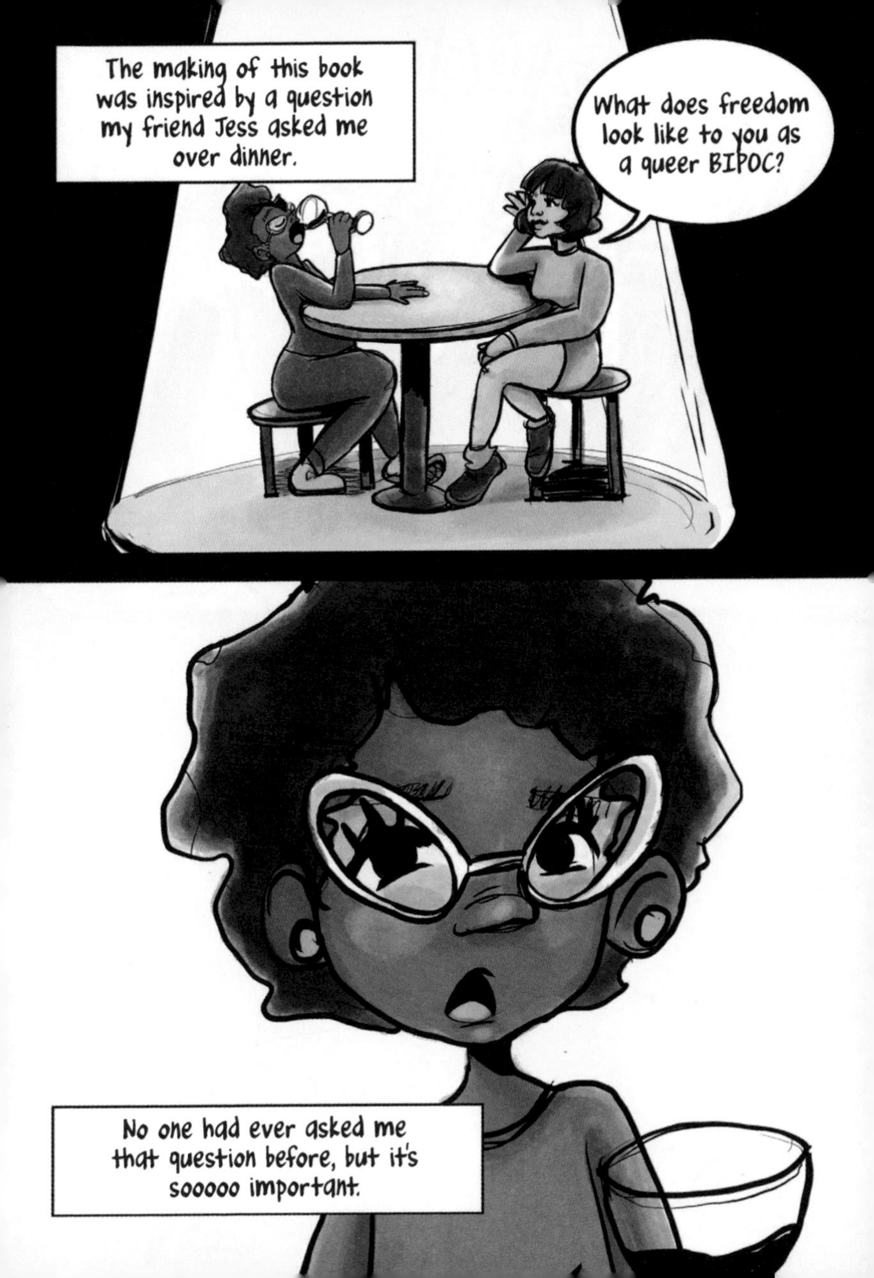

The making of this book was inspired by a question my friend Jess asked me over dinner.
What does freedom look like to you as a queer BIPOC?
No one had ever asked me that question before, but it's sooooo important.

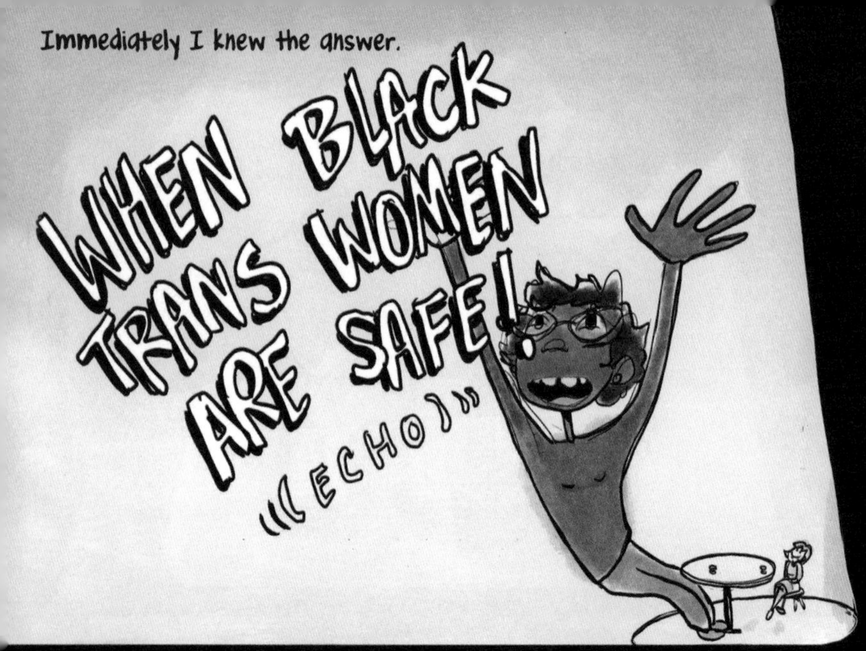
Immediately I knew the answer.
WHEN BLACK TRANS WOMEN ARE SAFE!
((ECHO))

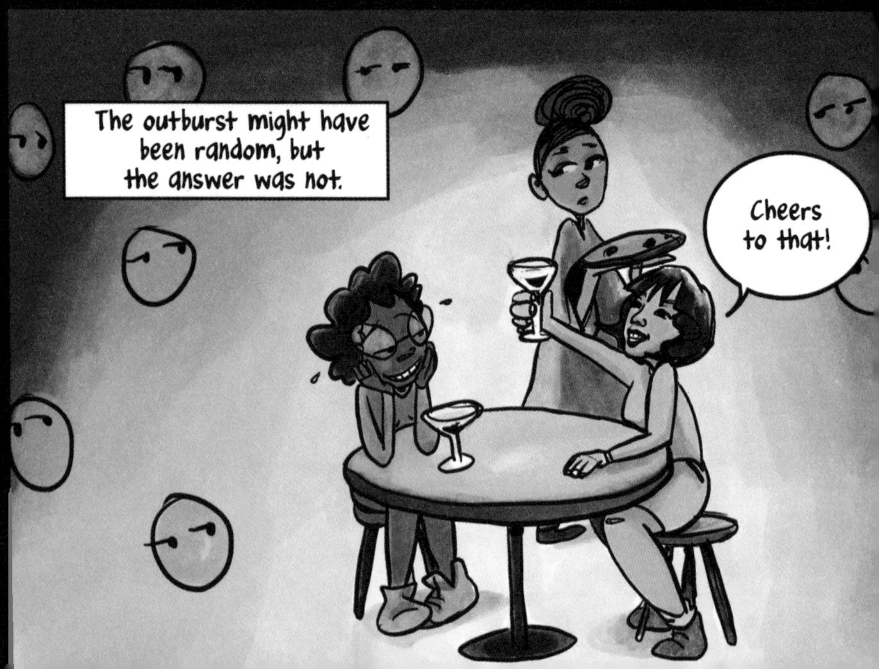
The outburst might have been random, but the answer was not.
Cheers to that!

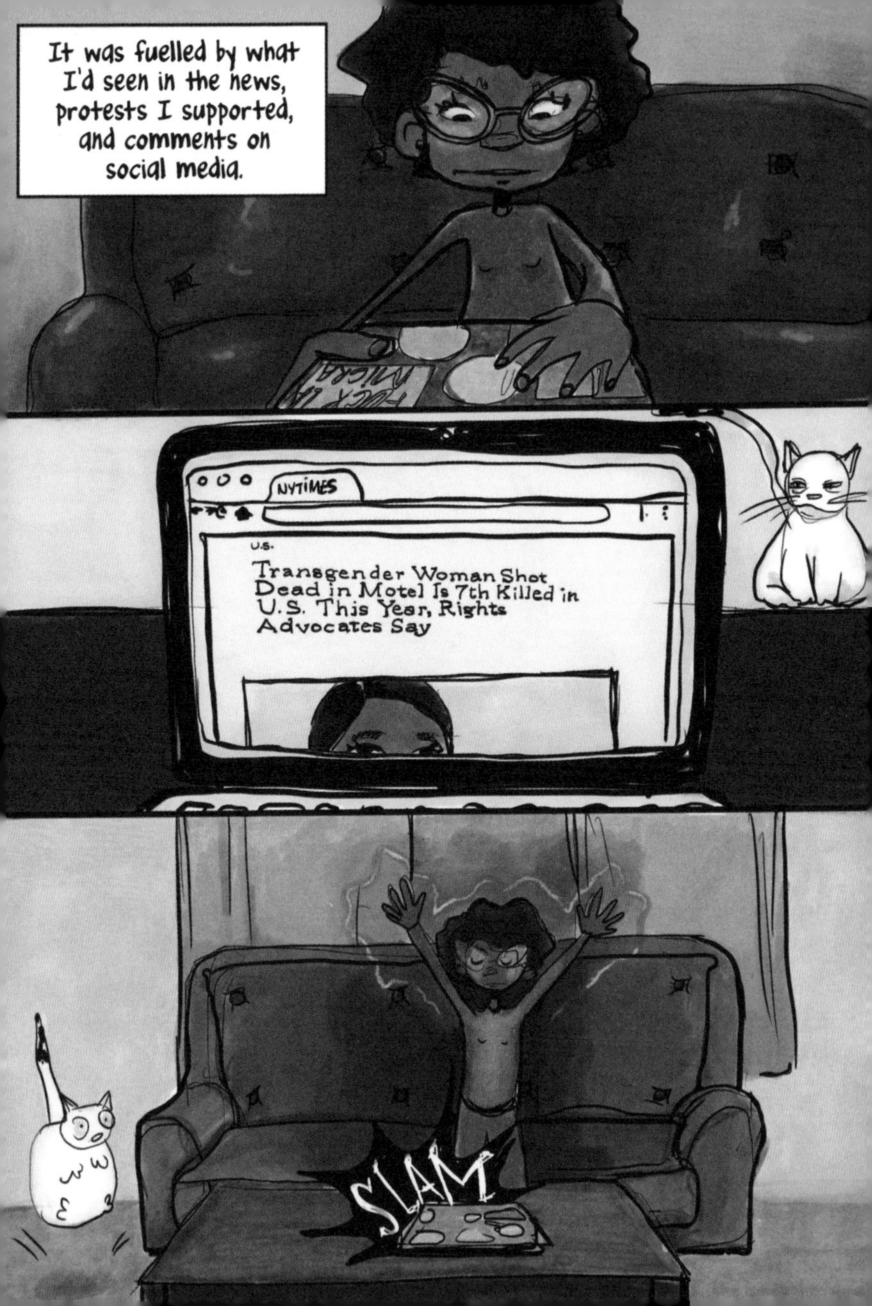
It was fuelled by what I'd seen in the news, protests I supported, and comments on social media.
NYTIMES
U.S.
Transgender Woman Shot Dead in Motel Is 7th Killed in U.S. This Year, Rights Advocates Say
SLAM

My answer was rooted in very complicated conversations with friends who have revealed homophobic feelings.

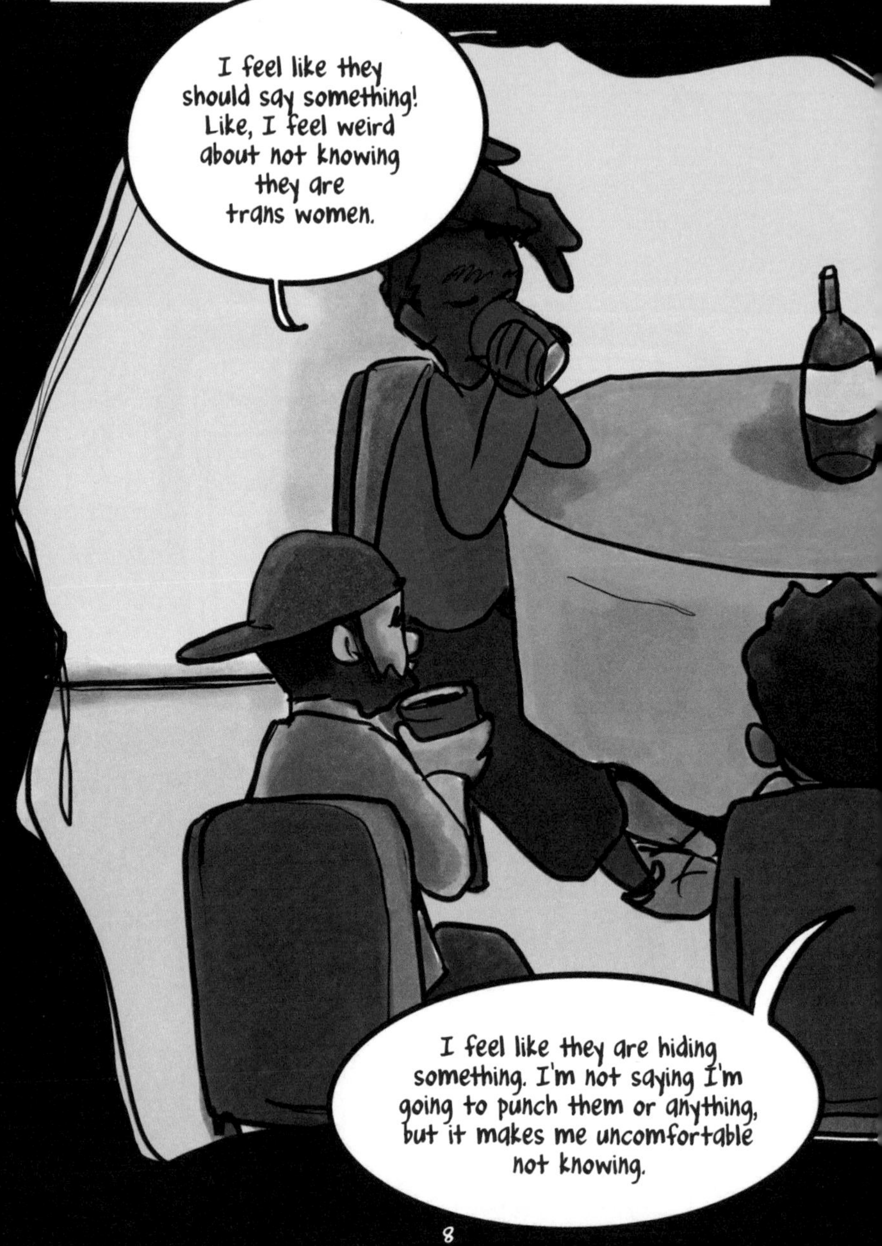
I feel like they should say something! Like, I feel weird about not knowing they are trans women.
I feel like they are hiding something. I'm not saying I'm going to punch them or anything, but it makes me uncomfortable not knowing.

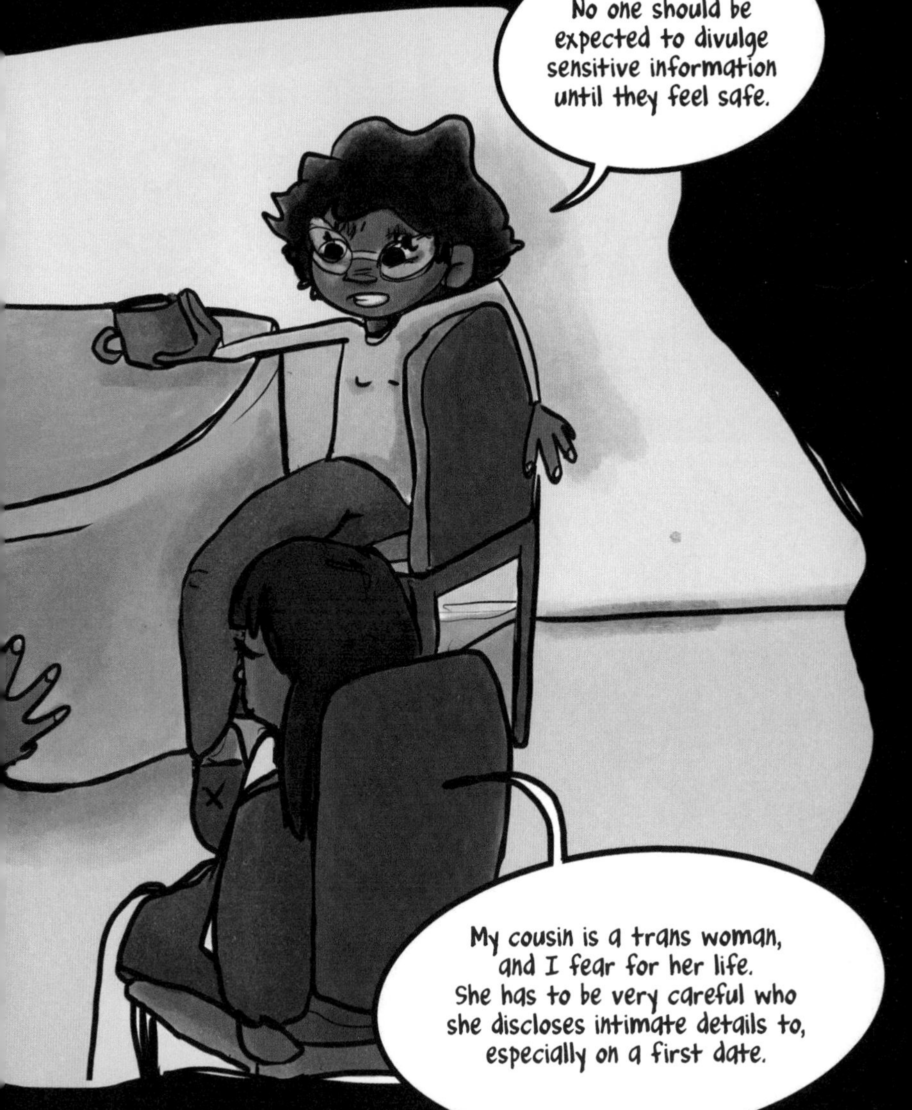
No one should be expected to divulge sensitive information until they feel safe.
My cousin is a trans woman, and I fear for her life. She has to be very careful who she discloses intimate details to, especially on a first date.

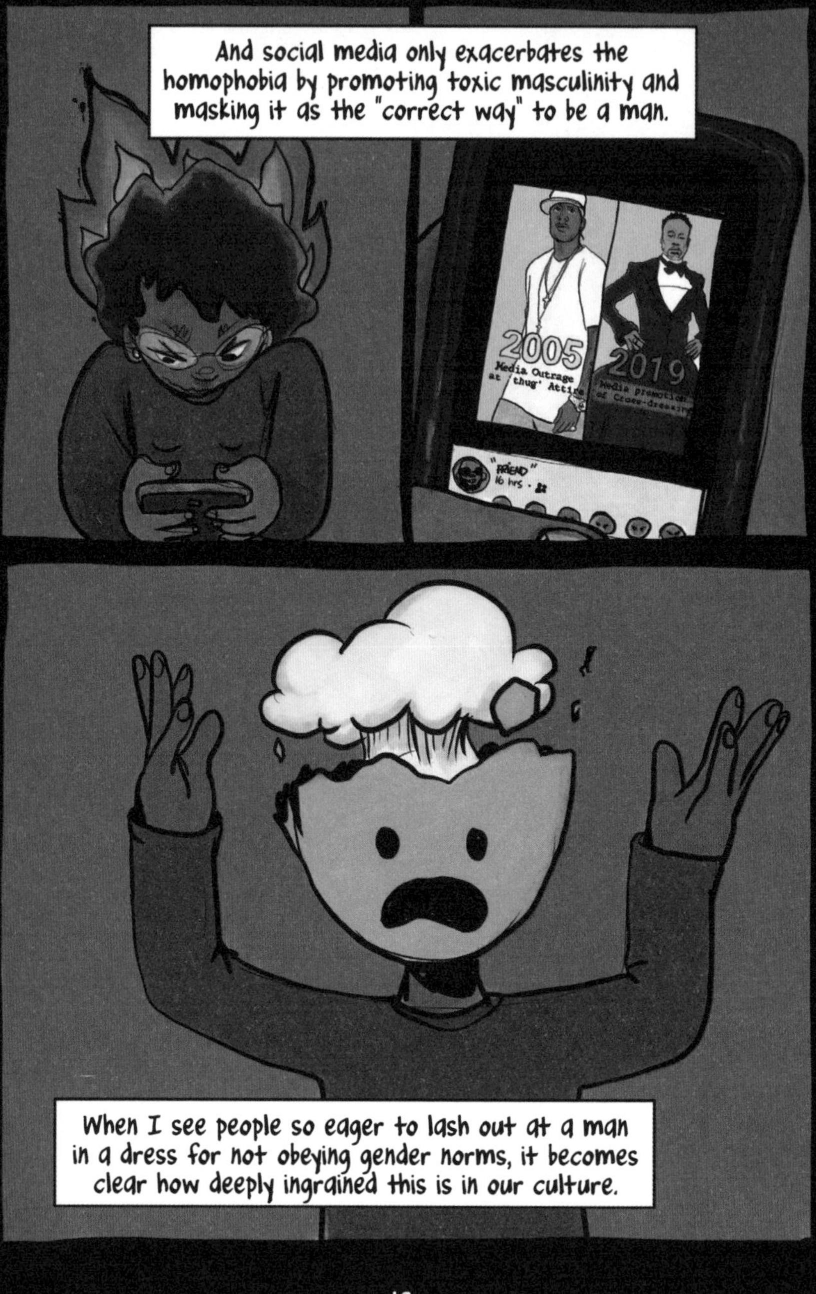
And social media only exacerbates the homophobia by promoting toxic masculinity and masking it as the "correct way" to be a man.
2005
Media Outrage
at 'thug' Attire
2019
When I see people so eager to lash out at a man in a dress for not obeying gender norms, it becomes clear how deeply ingrained this is in our culture.

Patriarchy thrives under strict gender norms, and toxic masculinity stems from patriarchy. Those "gender norms" assume behavior based on the gender you were assigned at birth. It's silly, because some days I feel masculine and other days I feel more feminine. Gender and sex are not interchangeable and anyway . . .

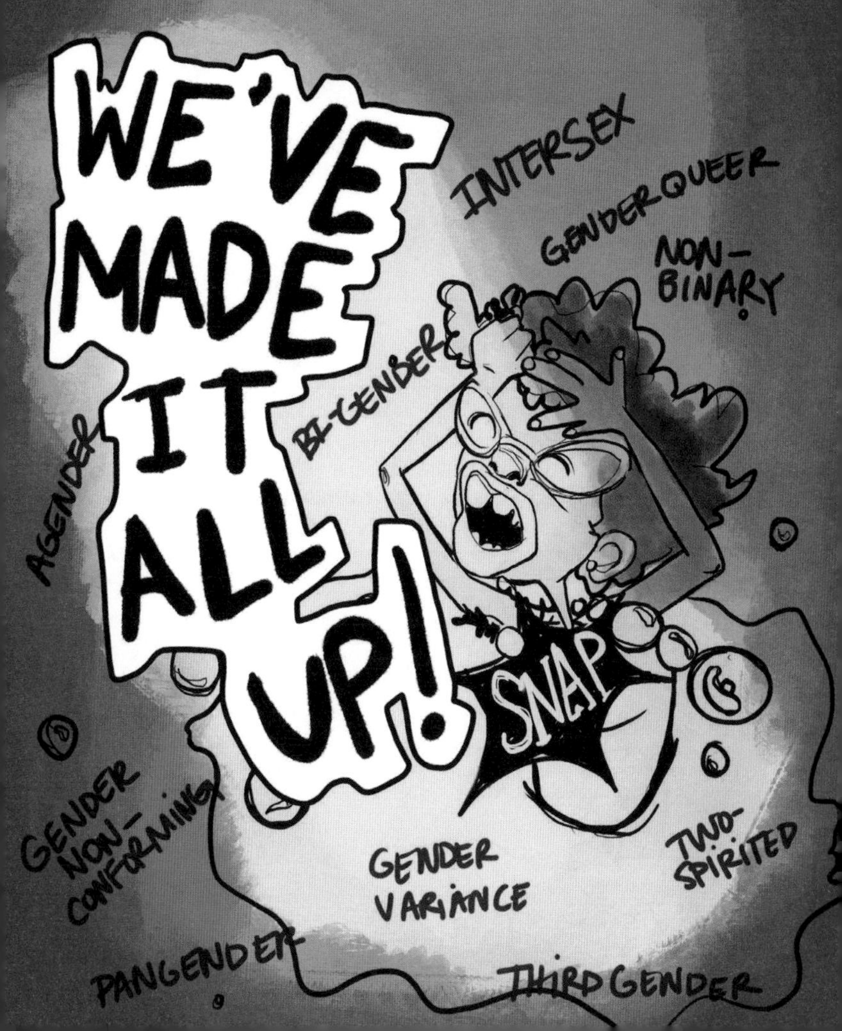
WE'VE MADE IT ALL UP!
INTERSEX
GENDERQUEER
NON-BINARY
BI-GENDER
AGENDER
SNAP
GENDER NON-CONFORMING
GENDER VARIANCE
TWO-SPIRITED
PANGENDER
THIRD GENDER

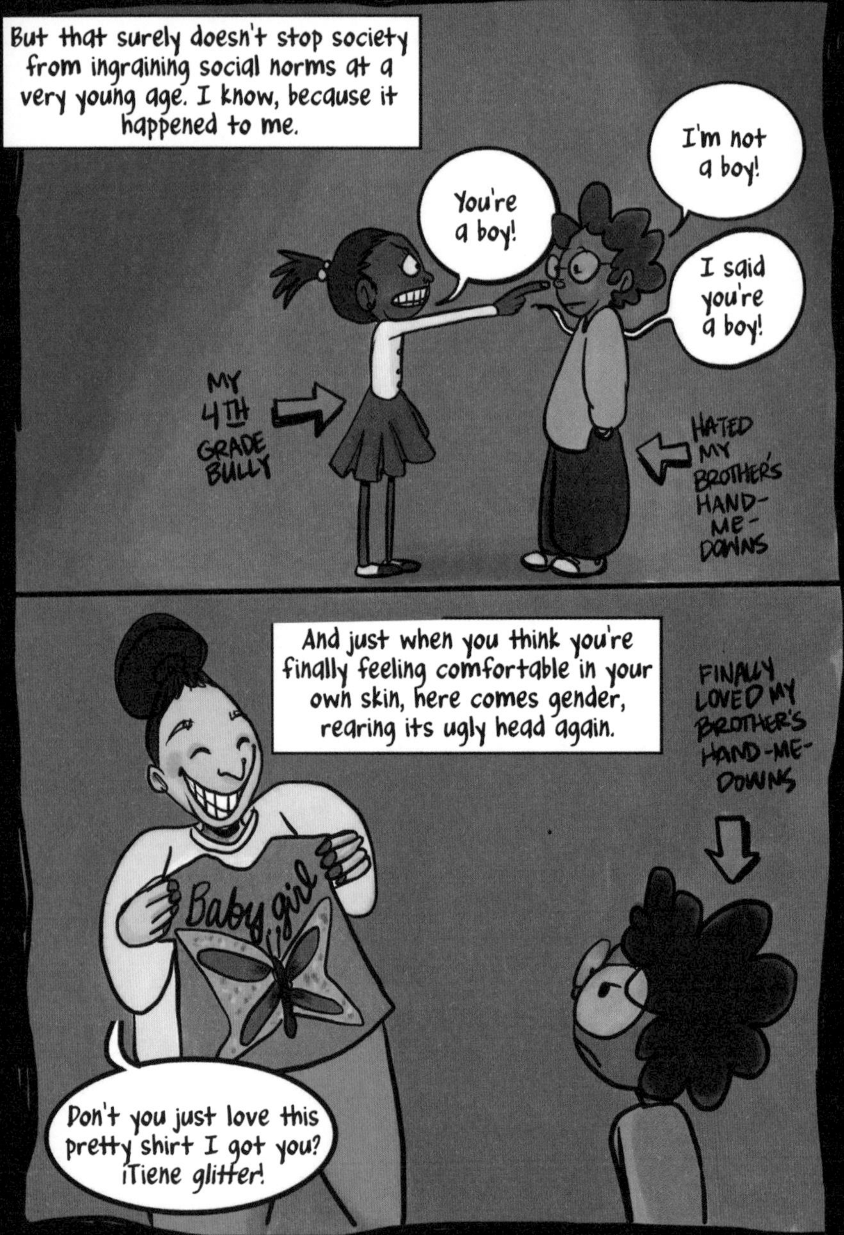

But that surely doesn't stop society from ingraining social norms at a very young age. I know, because it happened to me.
You're a boy!
I'm not a boy!
I said you're a boy!
MY 4TH GRADE BULLY
HATED MY BROTHER'S HAND-ME-DOWNS
And just when you think you're finally feeling comfortable in your own skin, here comes gender, rearing its ugly head again.
FINALLY LOVED MY BROTHER'S HAND-ME-DOWNS
Baby girl
Don't you just love this pretty shirt I got you? ¡Tiene glitter!

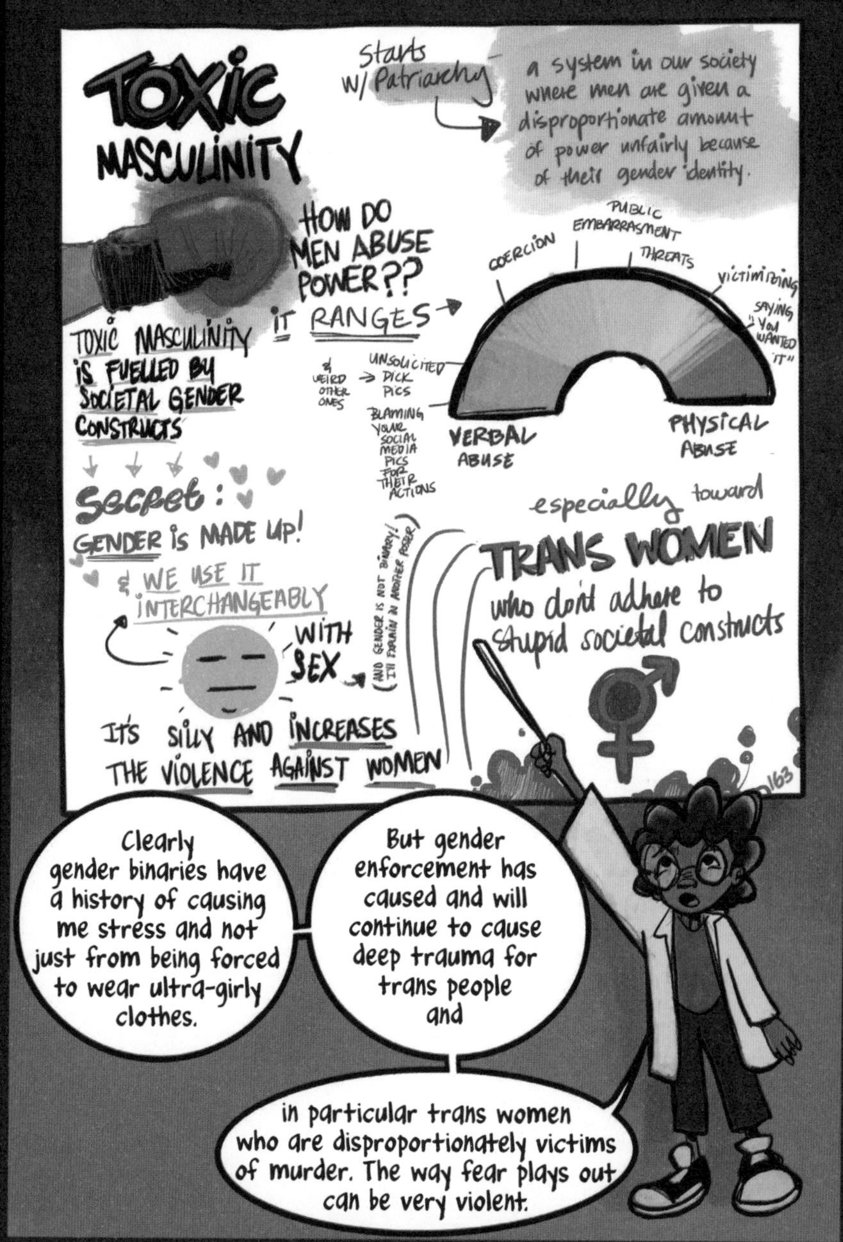

TOXIC MASCULINITY
Starts w/ Patriarchy
a system in our society where men are given a disproportionate amount of power unfairly because of their gender identity.
HOW DO MEN ABUSE POWER??
IT RANGES
COERCION
PUBLIC EMBARRASMENT
THREATS
VICTIMIZING
SAYING "YOU WANTED IT"
& WEIRD OTHER ONES
UNSOLICITED DICK PICS
BLAMING YOUR SOCIAL MEDIA PICS FOR THEIR ACTIONS
VERBAL ABUSE
PHYSICAL ABUSE
TOXIC MASCULINITY IS FUELLED BY SOCIETAL GENDER CONSTRUCTS
Secret:
GENDER IS MADE UP!
& WE USE IT INTERCHANGEABLY WITH SEX
(AND GENDER IS NOT BINARY! I'll EXPLAIN IN ANOTHER POSTER)
IT'S SILLY AND INCREASES THE VIOLENCE AGAINST WOMEN
especially toward
TRANS WOMEN
who don't adhere to stupid societal constructs
163
Clearly gender binaries have a history of causing me stress and not just from being forced to wear ultra-girly clothes.
But gender enforcement has caused and will continue to cause deep trauma for trans people and
in particular trans women who are disproportionately victims of murder. The way fear plays out can be very violent.

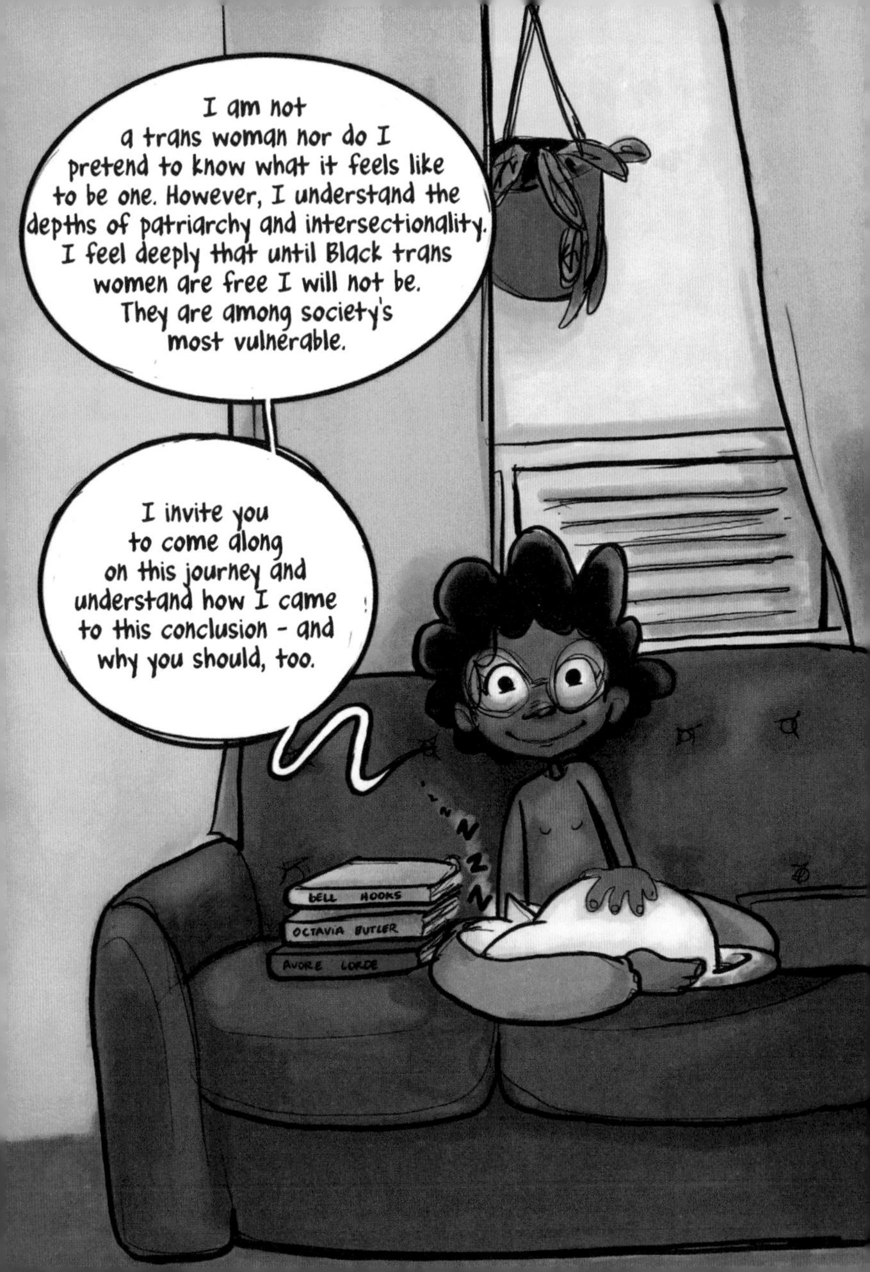
I am not a trans woman nor do I pretend to know what it feels like to be one. However, I understand the depths of patriarchy and intersectionality. I feel deeply that until Black trans women are free I will not be. They are among society's most vulnerable.
I invite you to come along on this journey and understand how I came to this conclusion - and why you should, too.
BELL HOOKS
OCTAVIA BUTLER
AUDRE LORDE
zzZZZ

2

xena

Although all of my early romantic relationships were with men, I have always been attracted to women. And not the "your skirt is cute" kind of attracted either.

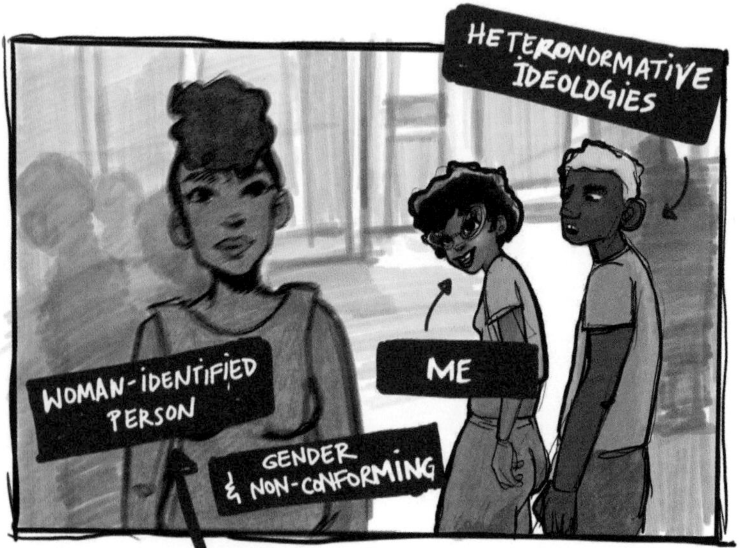
HETERONORMATIVE IDEOLOGIES
ME
WOMAN-IDENTIFIED PERSON
GENDER & NON-CONFORMING
THIS INCLUDES TRANS WOMEN (FOR ALL THE HATERS)

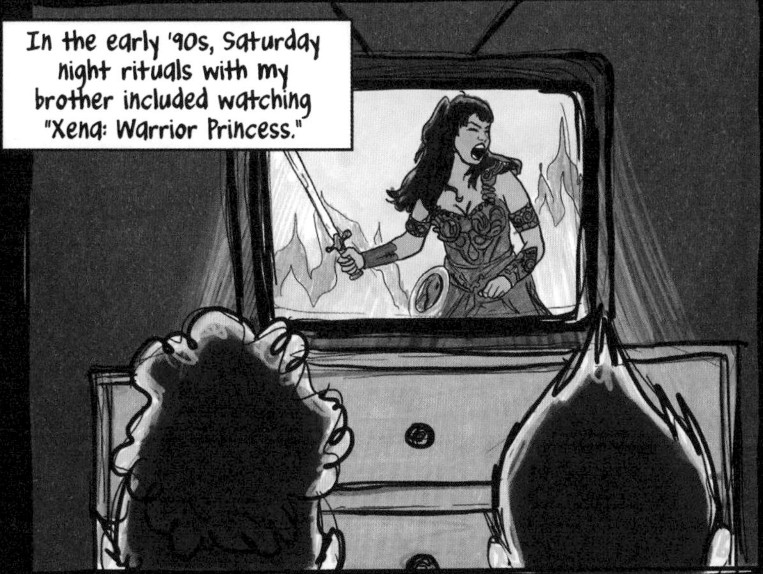
In the early '90s, Saturday night rituals with my brother included watching "Xena: Warrior Princess."

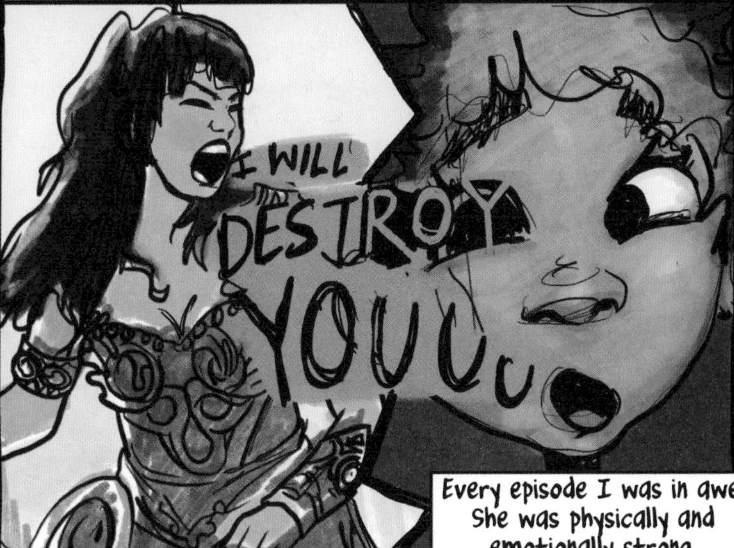
I WILL DESTROY YOUUUU
Every episode I was in awe. She was physically and emotionally strong, attractive, and a hero!

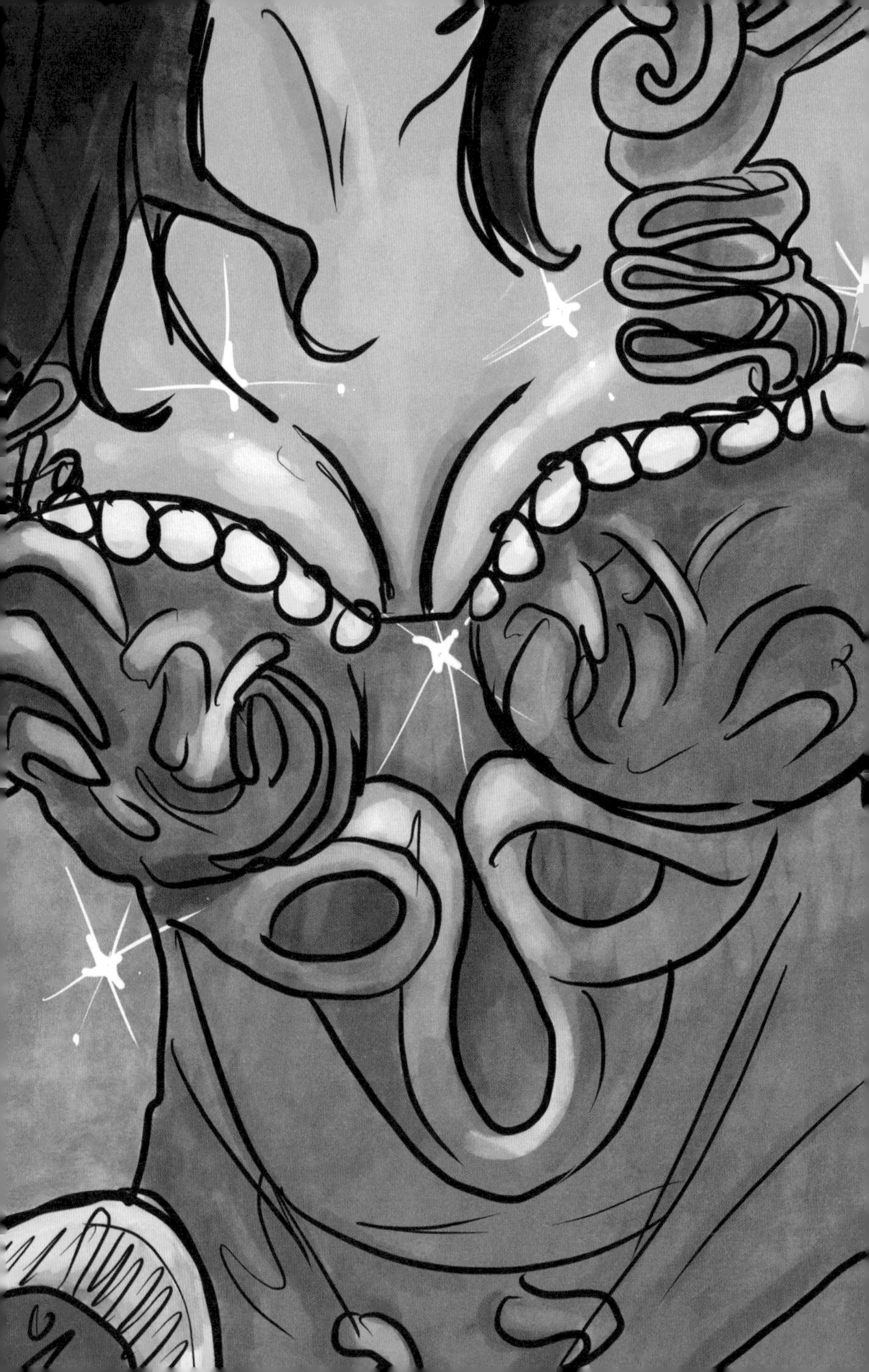

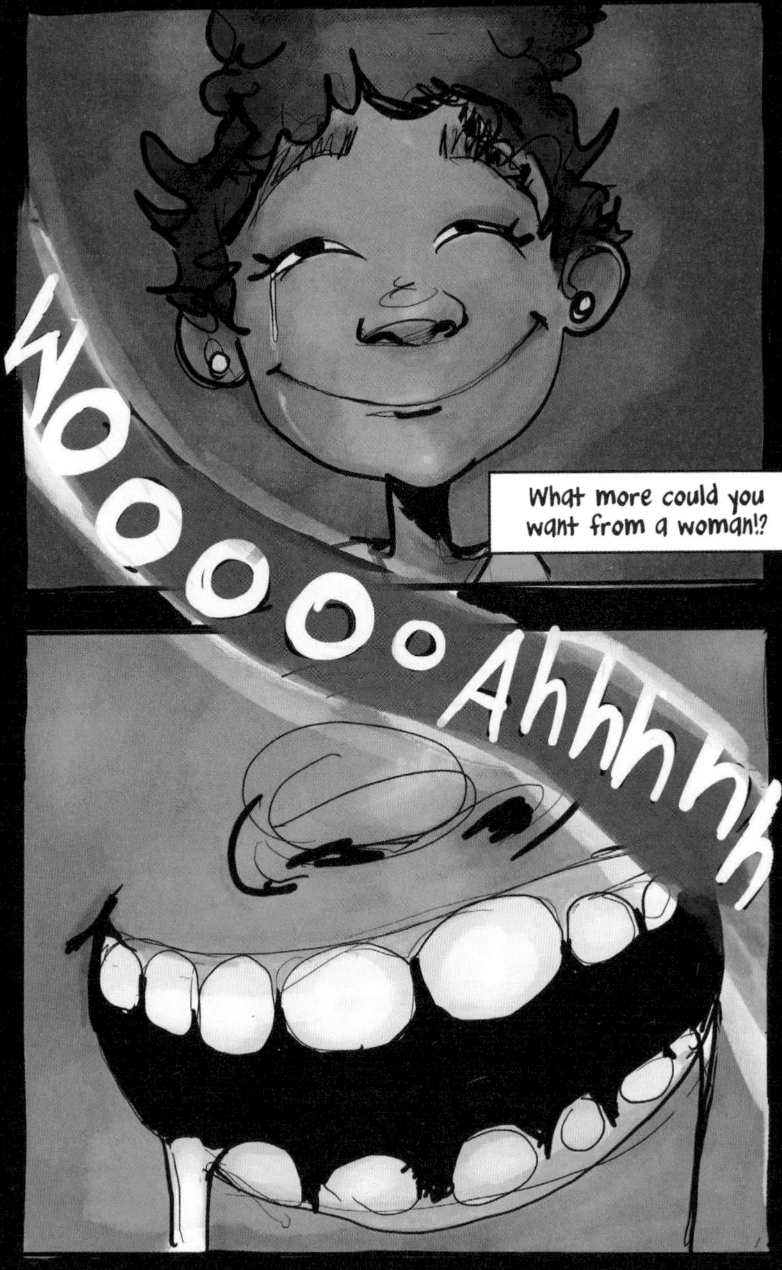
What more could you want from a woman!?
WOOOOOoAhhhhh

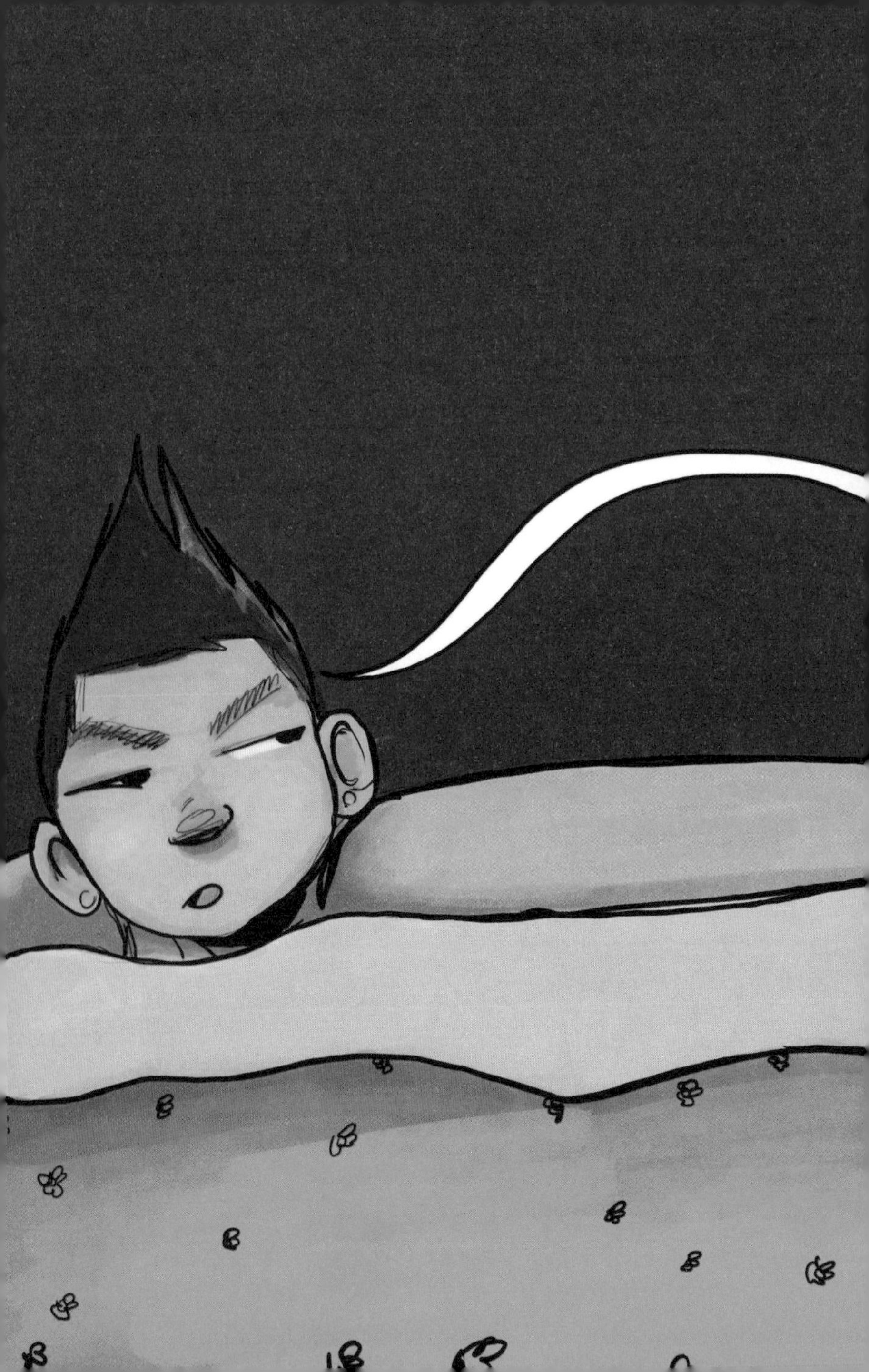

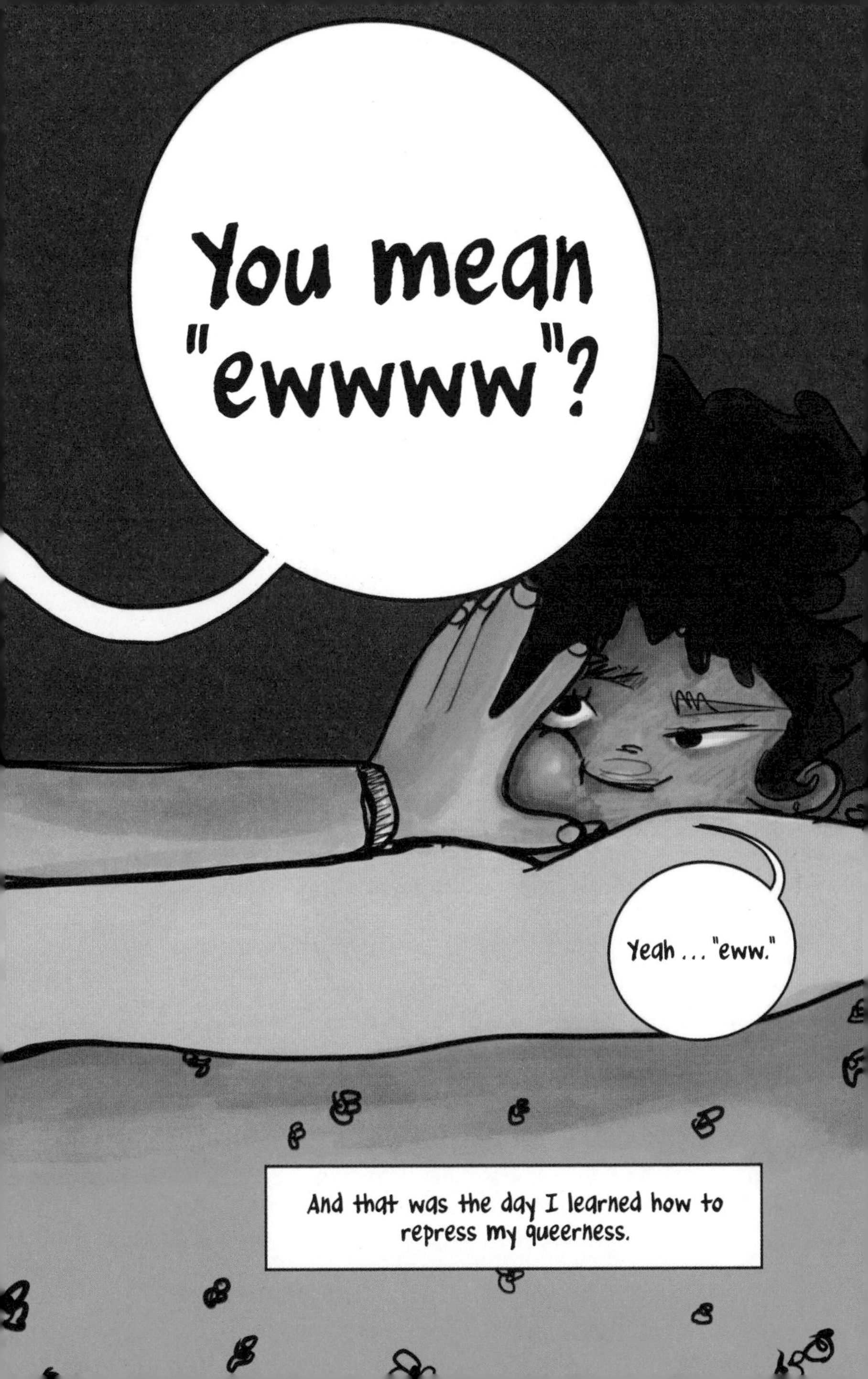
You mean "ewwww"?
Yeah . . . "eww."
And that was the day I learned how to repress my queerness.

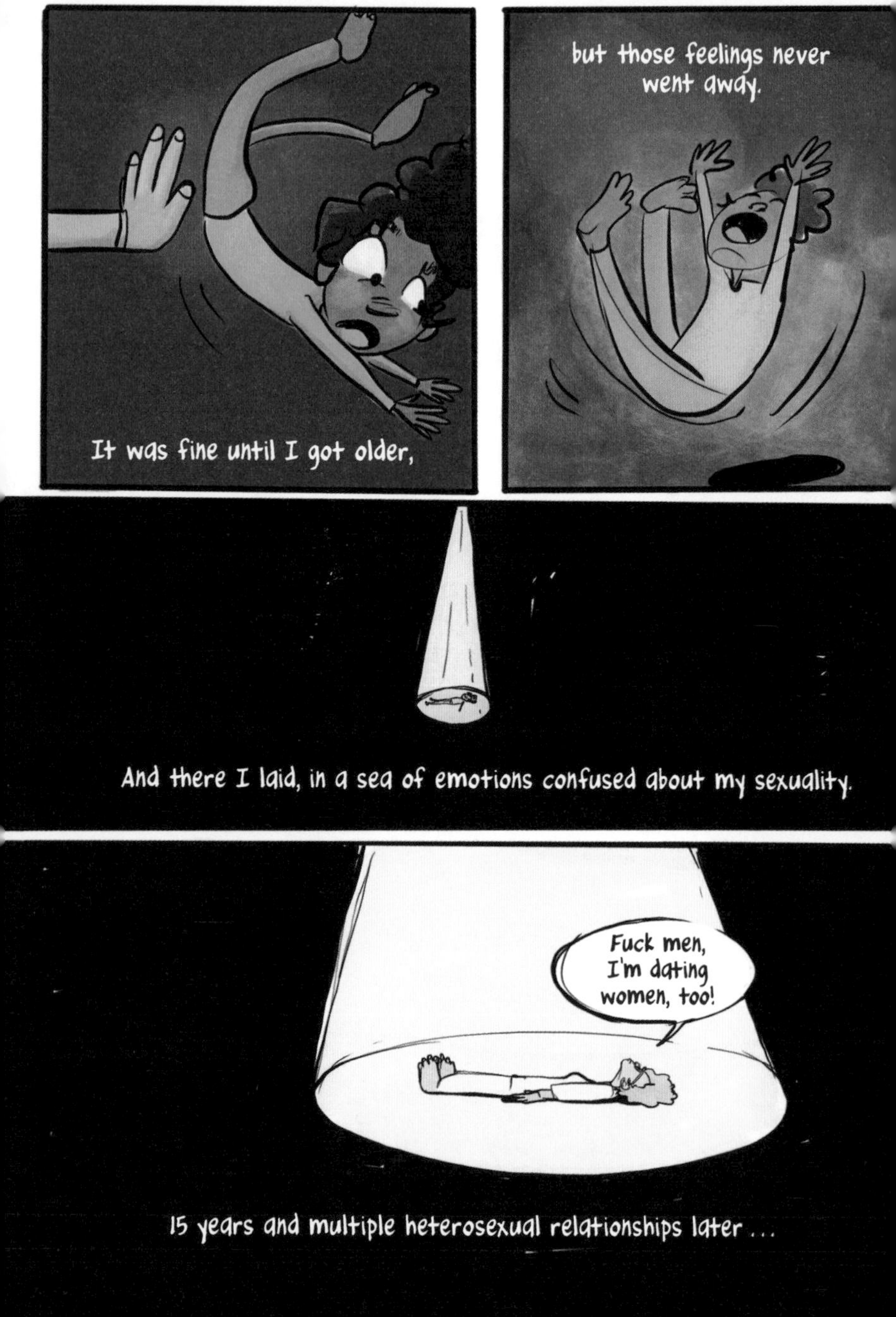
It was fine until I got older,
but those feelings never went away.
And there I laid, in a sea of emotions confused about my sexuality.
Fuck men, I'm dating women, too!
15 years and multiple heterosexual relationships later ...

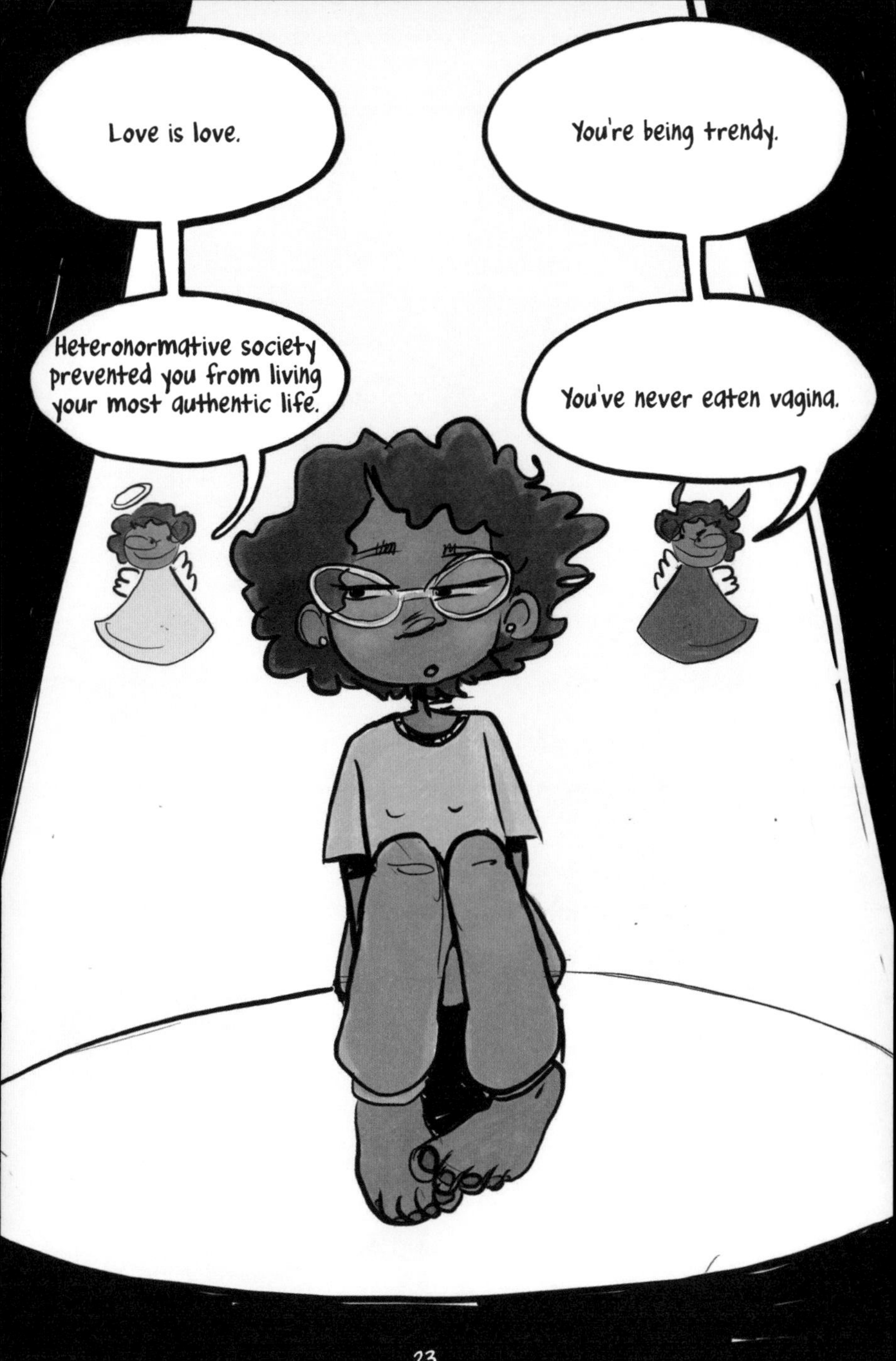
Love is love.
You're being trendy.
Heteronormative society prevented you from living your most authentic life.
You've never eaten vagina.

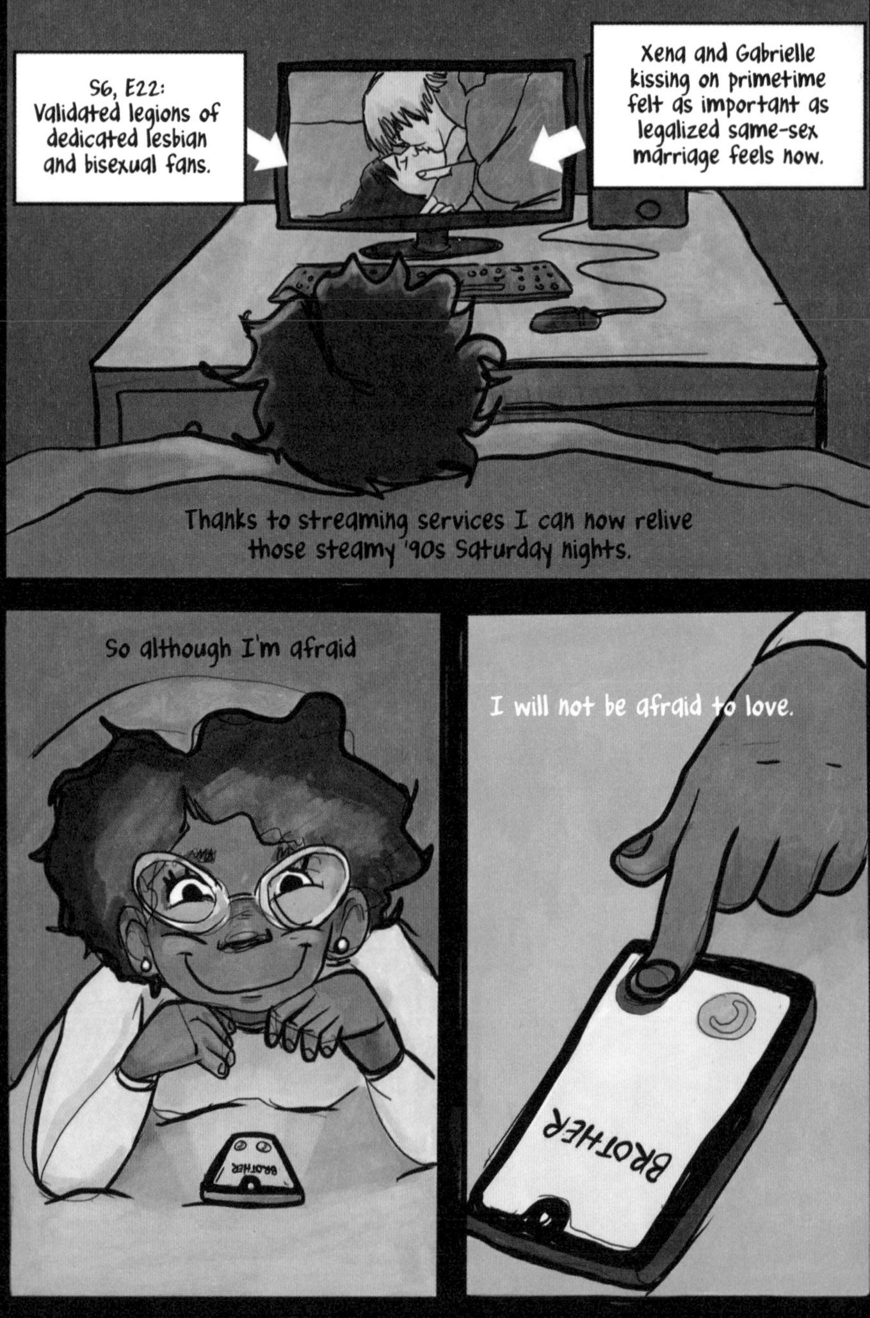
S6, E22:
Validated legions of dedicated lesbian and bisexual fans.
Xena and Gabrielle kissing on primetime felt as important as legalized same-sex marriage feels now.
Thanks to streaming services I can now relive those steamy '90s Saturday nights.
So although I'm afraid
BROTHER
I will not be afraid to love.
BROTHER

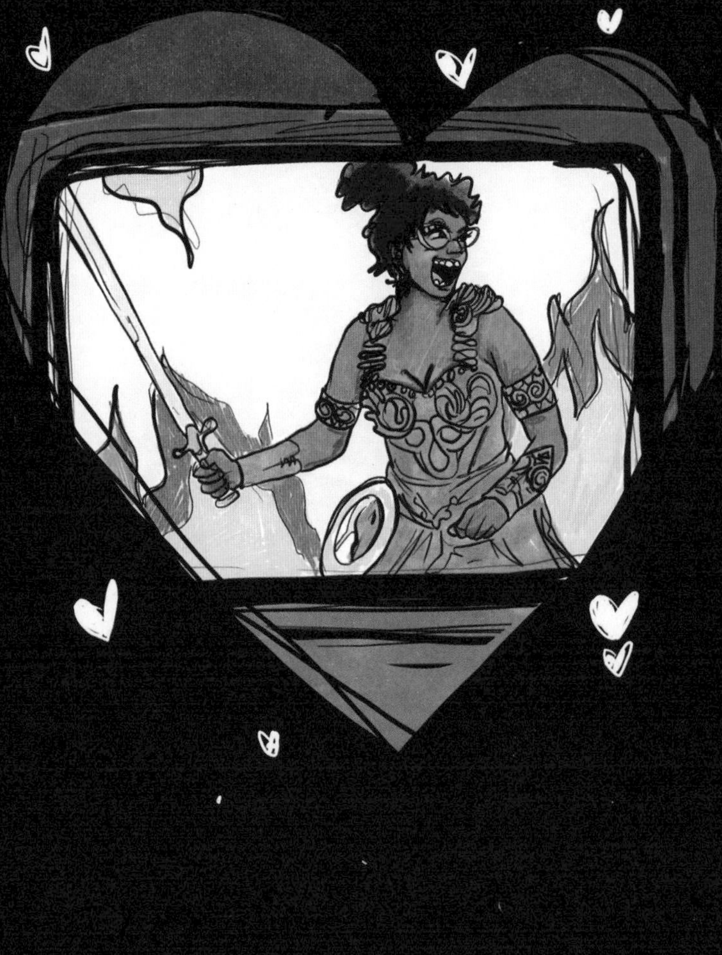

DISCLAIMER: I've eaten vagina and I like it.

3
Queer
Spaces

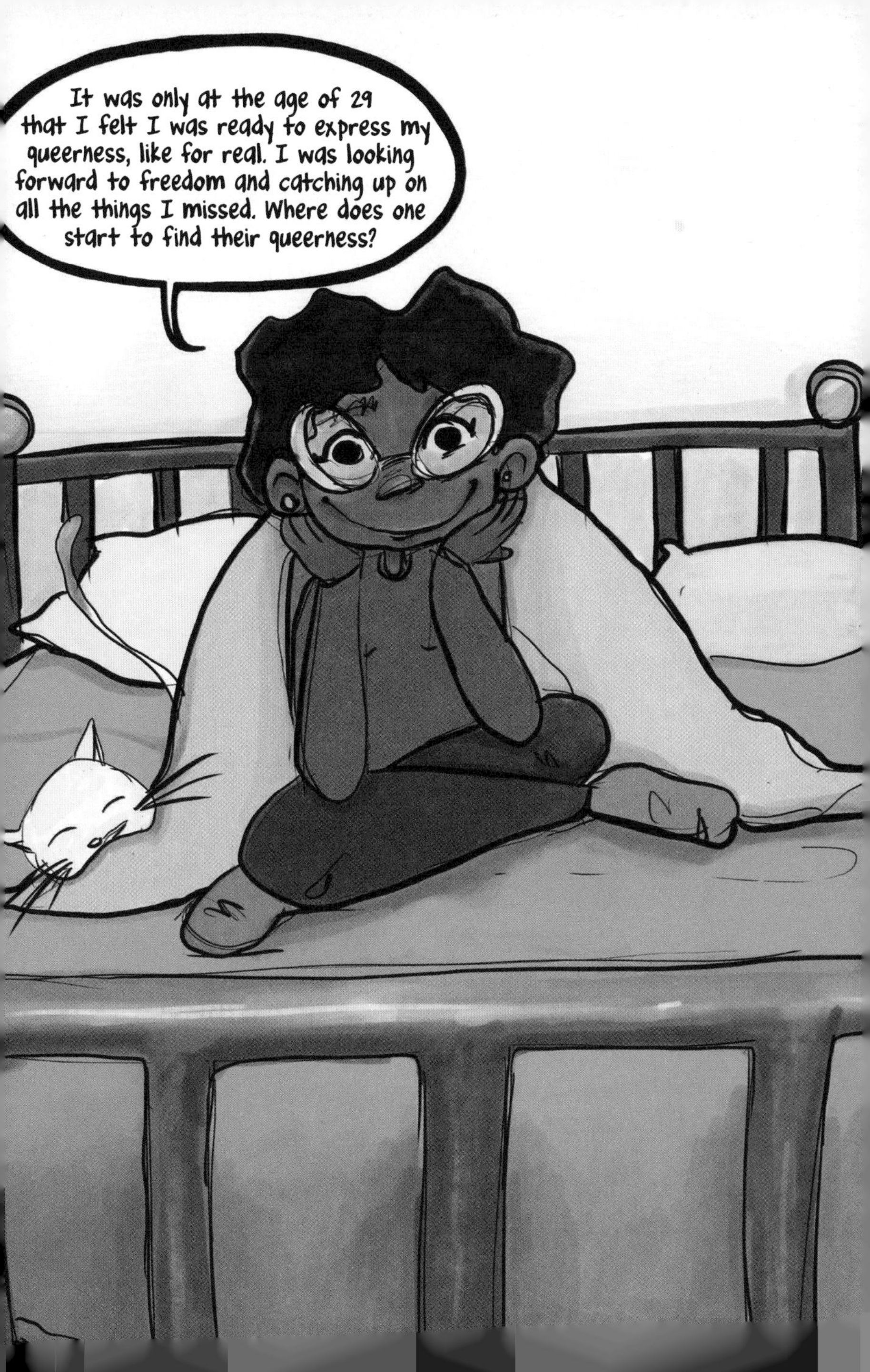
It was only at the age of 29 that I felt I was ready to express my queerness, like for real. I was looking forward to freedom and catching up on all the things I missed. Where does one start to find their queerness?

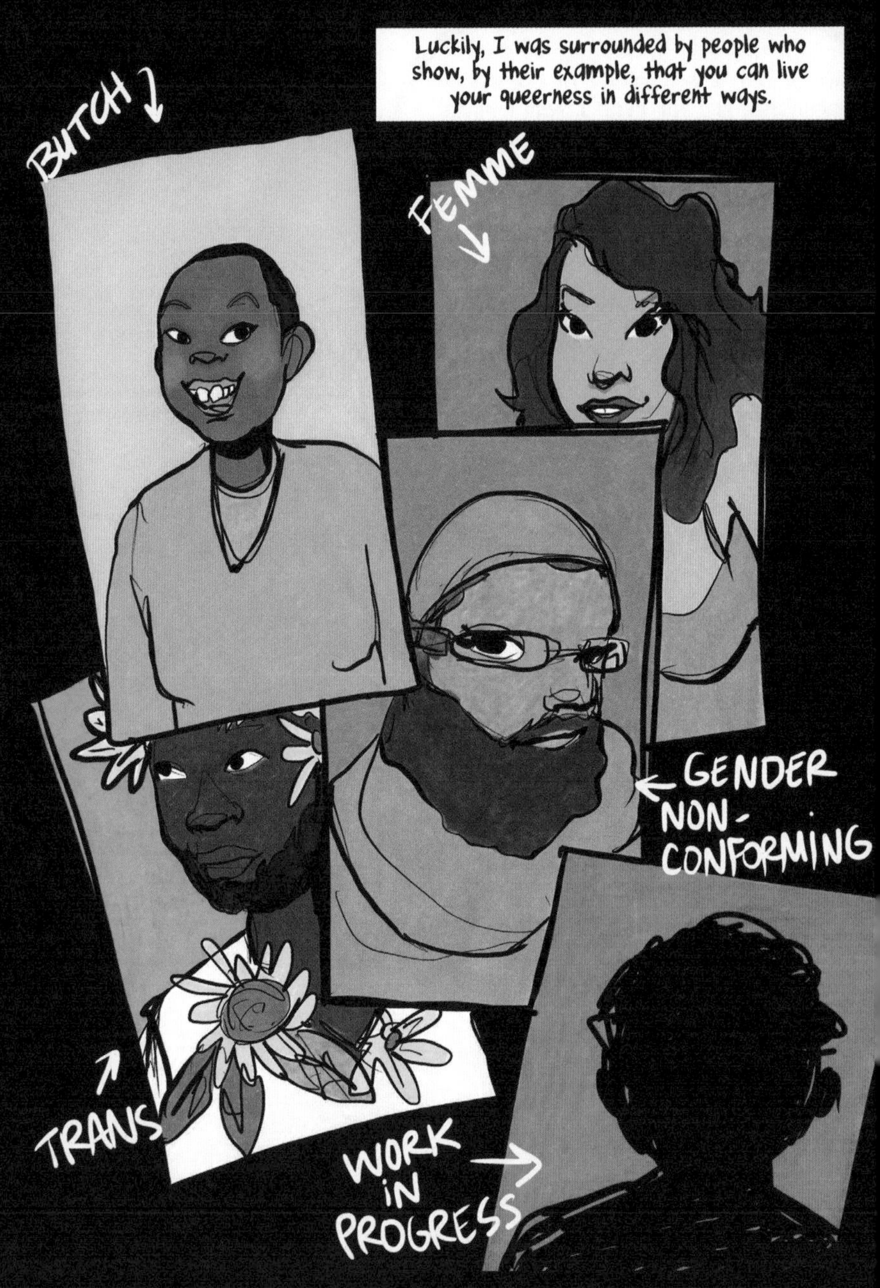

Luckily, I was surrounded by people who show, by their example, that you can live your queerness in different ways.
BUTCH
FEMME
GENDER NON-CONFORMING
TRANS
WORK IN PROGRESS

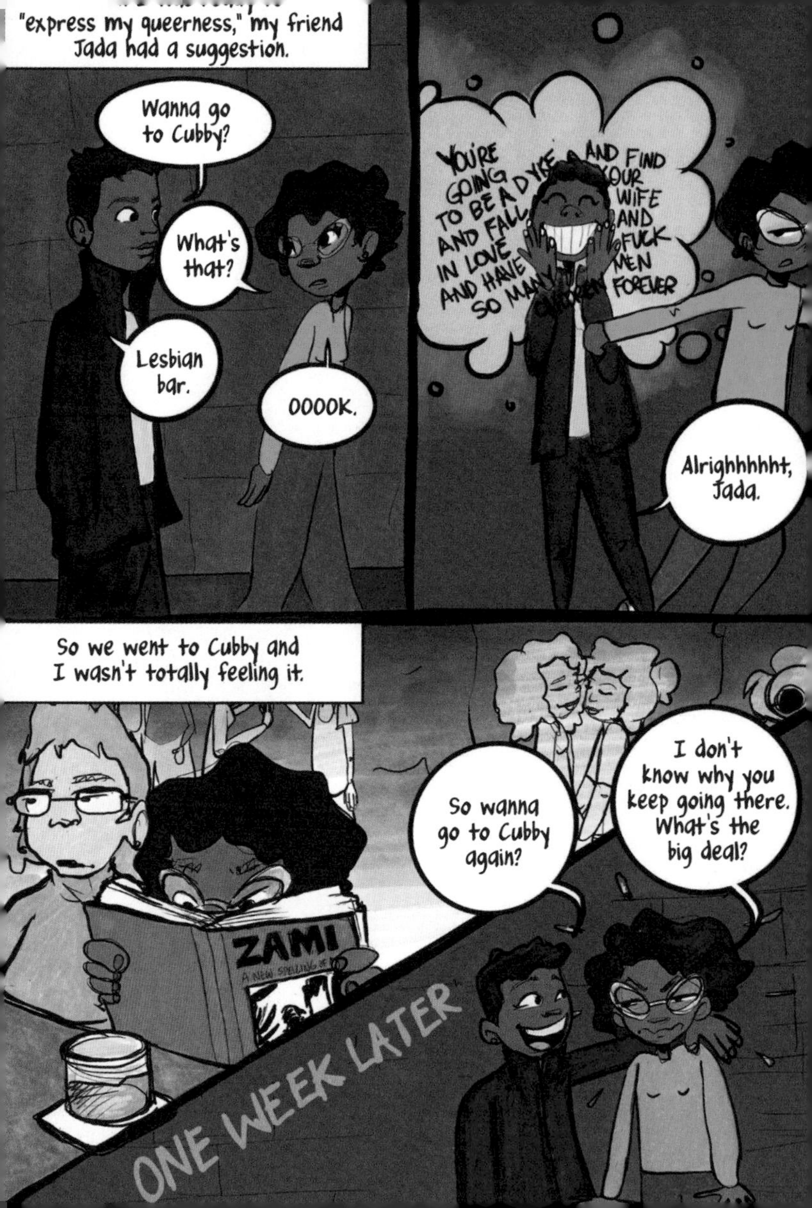
"express my queerness," my friend Jada had a suggestion.
Wanna go to Cubby?
What's that?
Lesbian bar.
OOOOK.
YOU'RE GOING TO BE A DYKE AND FALL IN LOVE AND HAVE SO MANY
AND FIND YOUR WIFE AND FUCK MEN FOREVER
Alrighhhhht, Jada.
So we went to Cubby and I wasn't totally feeling it.
ZAMI
ONE WEEK LATER
So wanna go to Cubby again?
I don't know why you keep going there. What's the big deal?

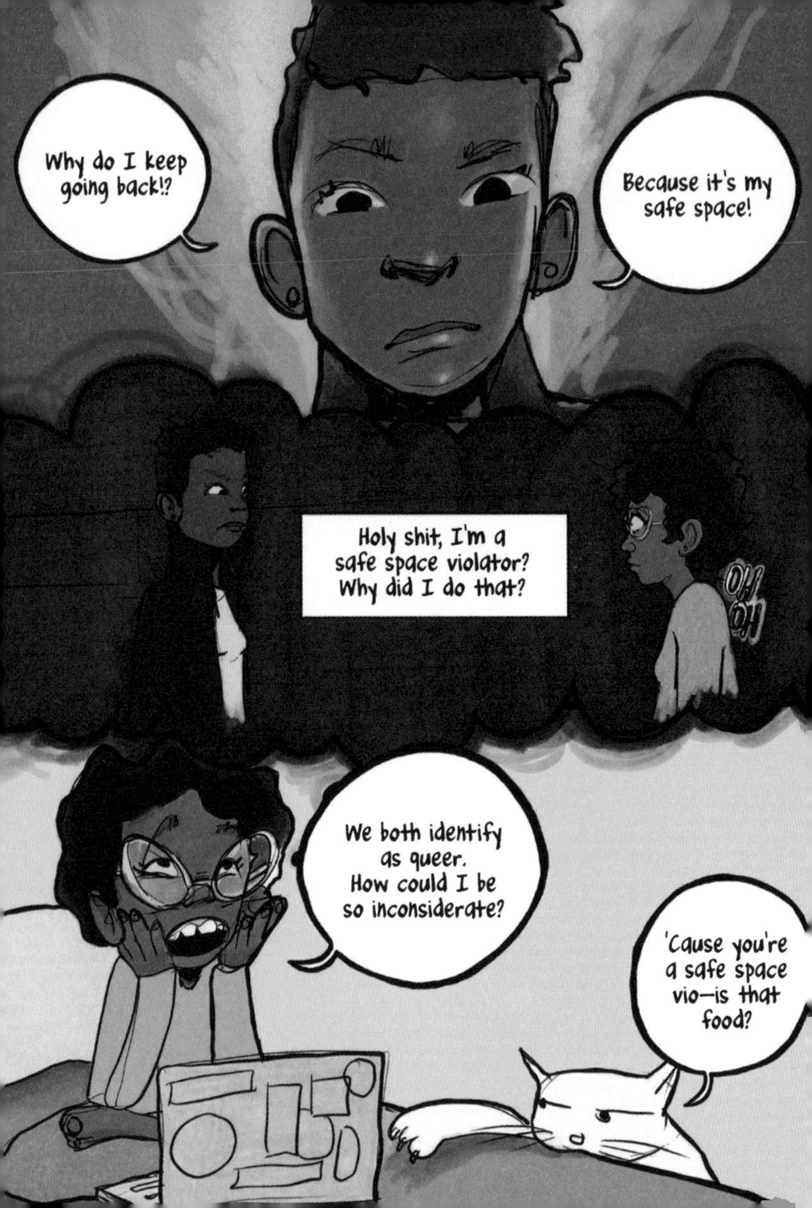
Why do I keep going back!?
Because it's my safe space!
Holy shit, I'm a safe space violator? Why did I do that?
OH HO
We both identify as queer. How could I be so inconsiderate?
'Cause you're a safe space vio—is that food?

I understood the importance of safe spaces for LGBTQIA+ folks, but I didn't think of a bar as a safe space for me. I had to revise this opinion. Getting some historical context helped.

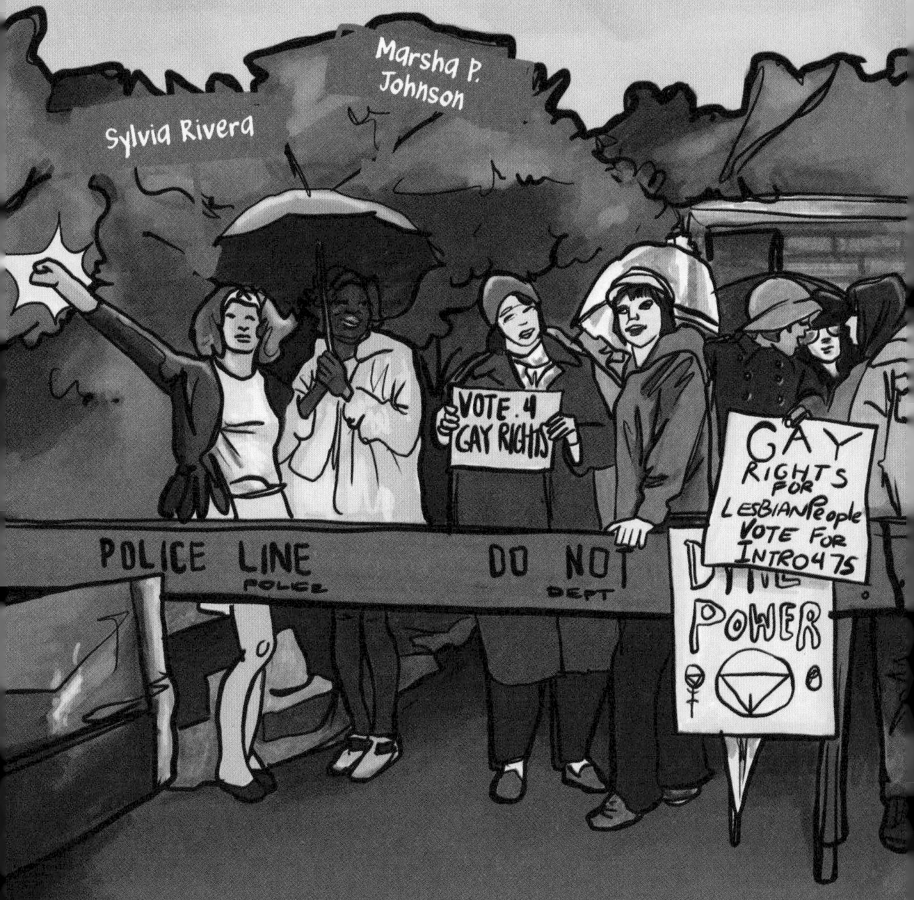

Sylvia Rivera
Marsha P. Johnson
VOTE 4 GAY RIGHTS
GAY RIGHTS FOR LESBIAN People VOTE FOR INTRO 475
POLICE LINE
POLICE
DO NOT
DEPT
POWER

Meet Sylvia Rivera and Marsha P. Johnson, two icons of queer liberation who went down in history for defending a queer space that just happened to be a bar — The Stonewall Inn. Starting in the 1850s cross-dressing laws became a tool of police harassment and, to no one's surprise, gender rebels were on the front lines.

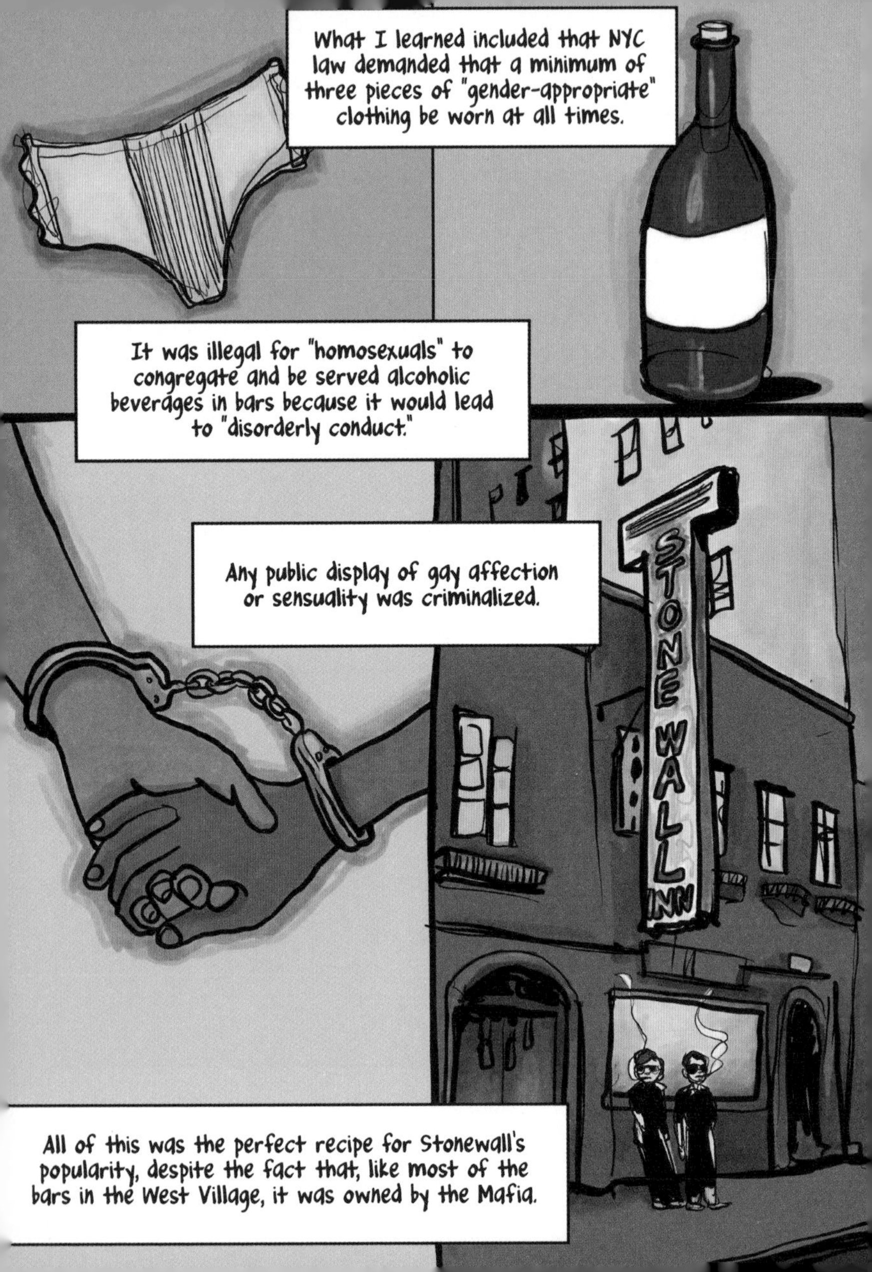
What I learned included that NYC law demanded that a minimum of three pieces of "gender-appropriate" clothing be worn at all times.
It was illegal for "homosexuals" to congregate and be served alcoholic beverages in bars because it would lead to "disorderly conduct."
Any public display of gay affection or sensuality was criminalized.
STONEWALL INN
All of this was the perfect recipe for Stonewall's popularity, despite the fact that, like most of the bars in the West Village, it was owned by the Mafia.

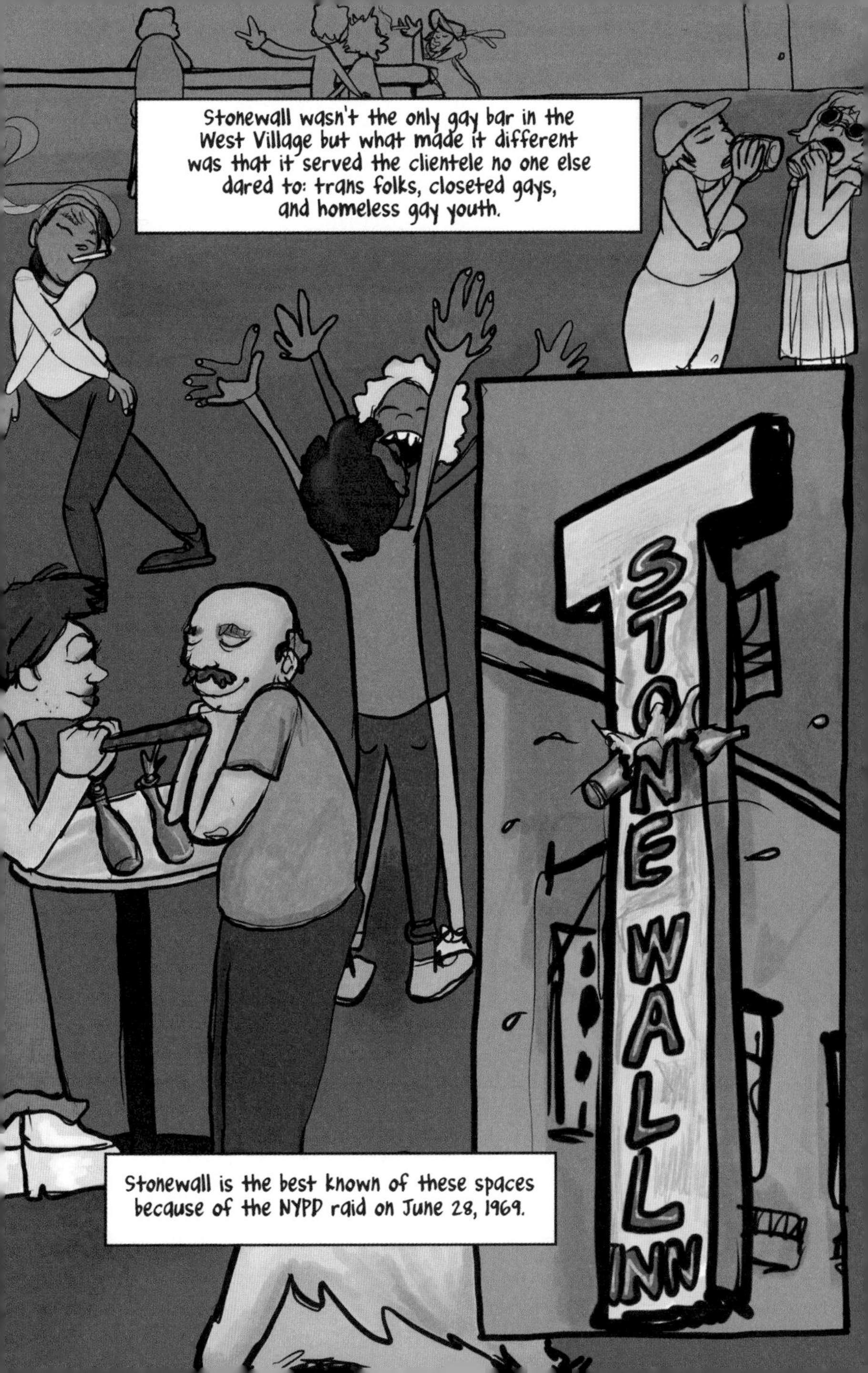
Stonewall wasn't the only gay bar in the West Village but what made it different was that it served the clientele no one else dared to: trans folks, closeted gays, and homeless gay youth.
Stonewall is the best known of these spaces because of the NYPD raid on June 28, 1969.
STONEWALL INN

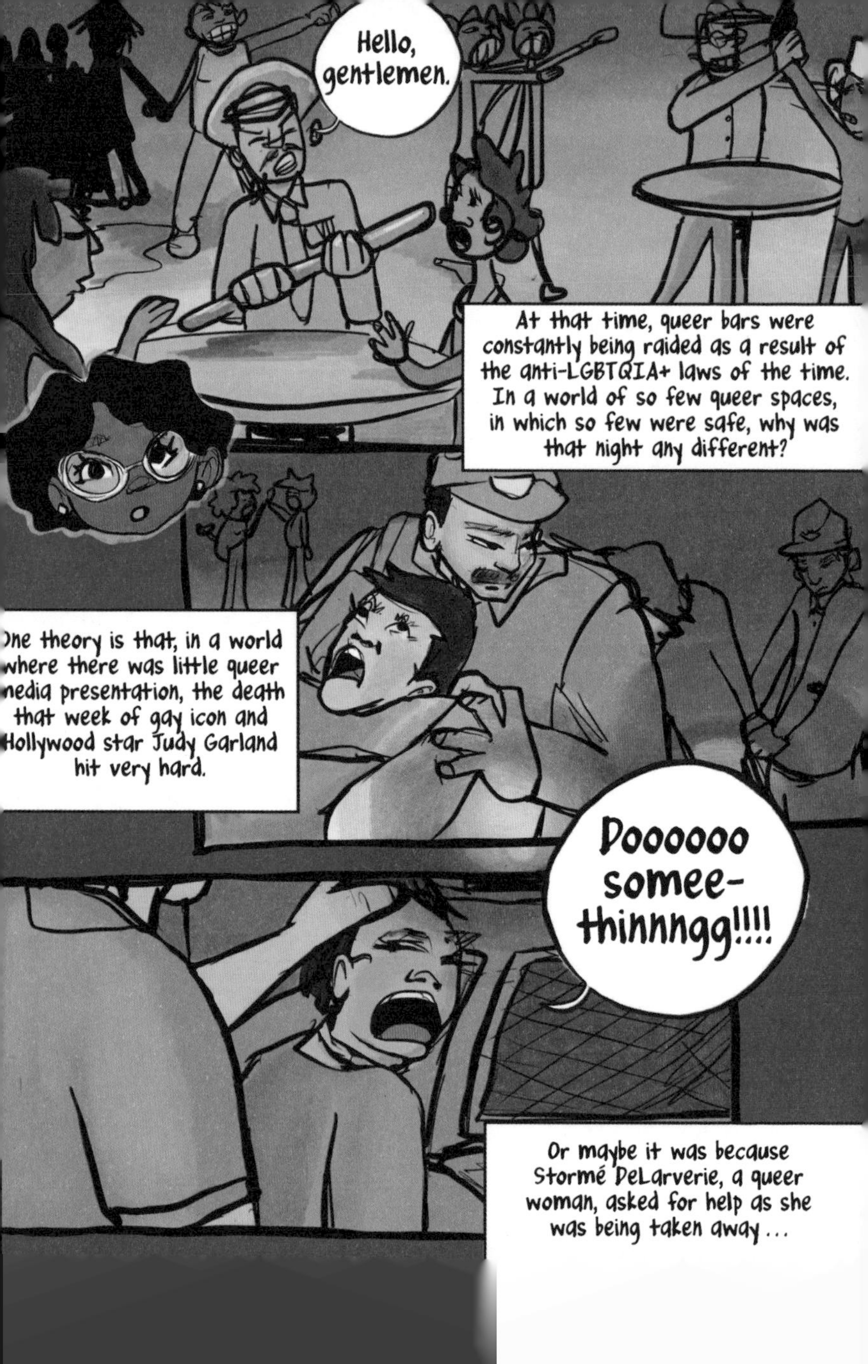
Hello, gentlemen.
At that time, queer bars were constantly being raided as a result of the anti-LGBTQIA+ laws of the time. In a world of so few queer spaces, in which so few were safe, why was that night any different?
One theory is that, in a world where there was little queer media presentation, the death that week of gay icon and Hollywood star Judy Garland hit very hard.
Doooooo somee-thinnngg!!!!
Or maybe it was because Stormé DeLarverie, a queer woman, asked for help as she was being taken away . . .

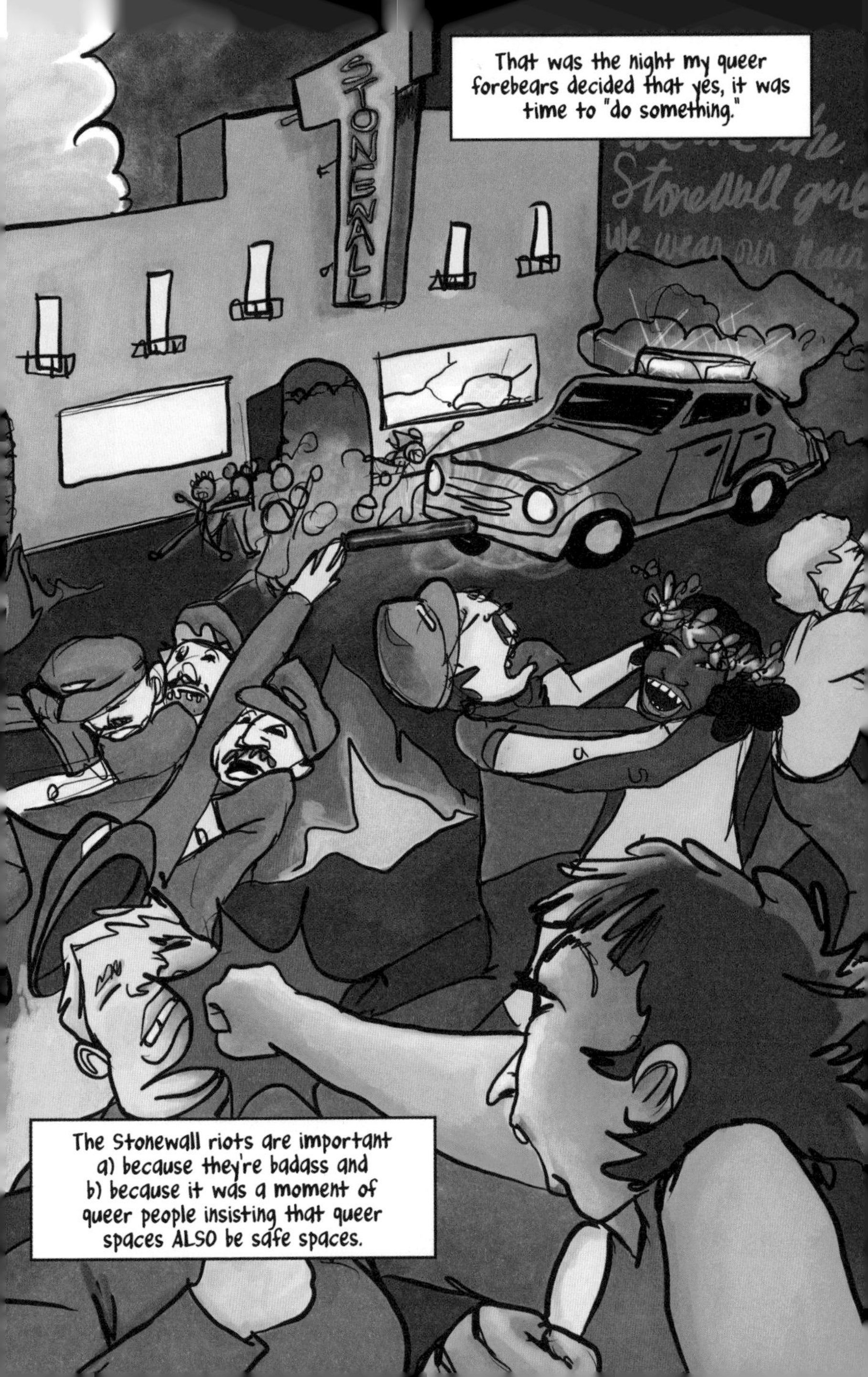
That was the night my queer forebears decided that yes, it was time to "do something."
STONEWALL
The Stonewall riots are important a) because they're badass and b) because it was a moment of queer people insisting that queer spaces ALSO be safe spaces.

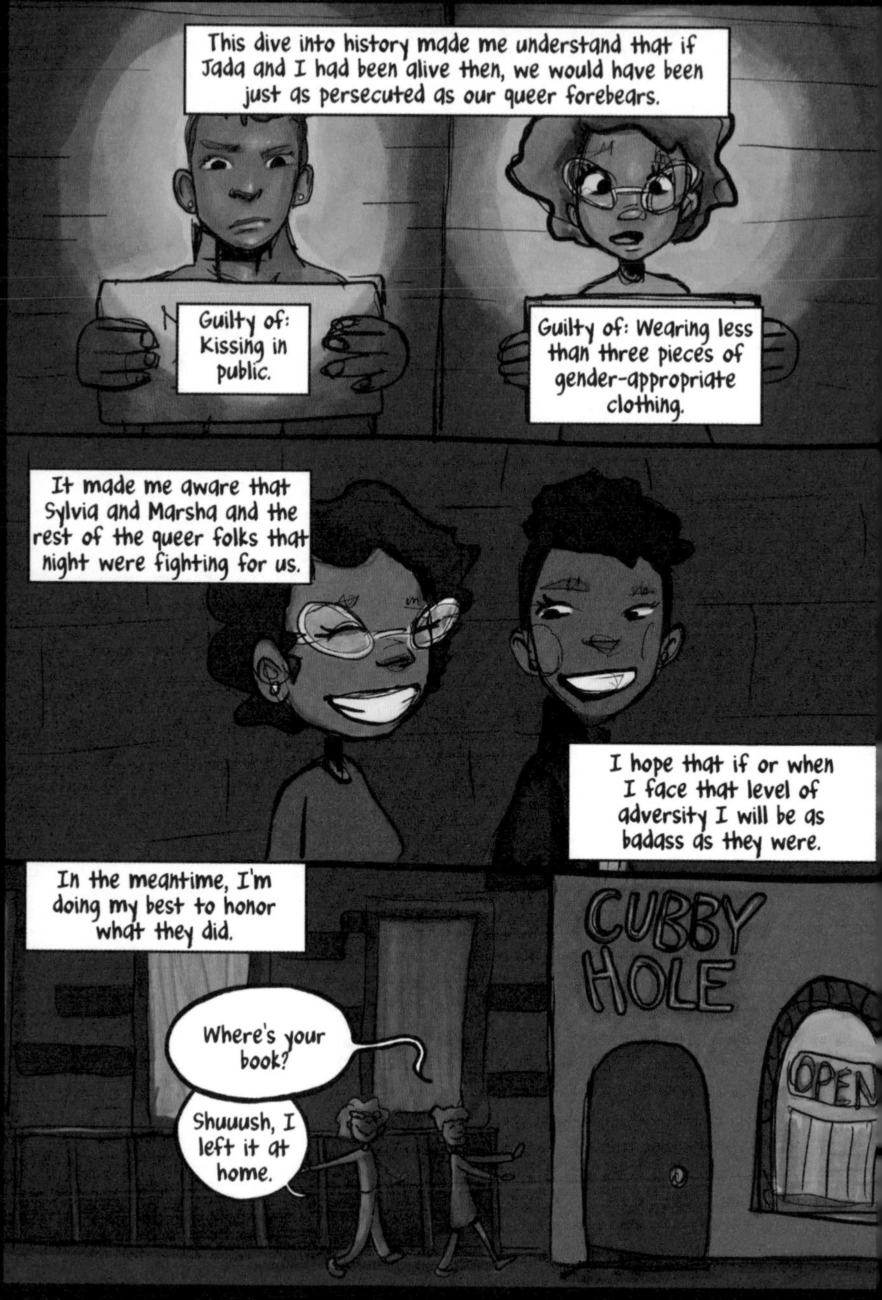
This dive into history made me understand that if Jada and I had been alive then, we would have been just as persecuted as our queer forebears.
Guilty of: Kissing in public.
Guilty of: Wearing less than three pieces of gender-appropriate clothing.
It made me aware that Sylvia and Marsha and the rest of the queer folks that night were fighting for us.
I hope that if or when I face that level of adversity I will be as badass as they were.
In the meantime, I'm doing my best to honor what they did.
CUBBY HOLE
OPEN
Where's your book?
Shuuush, I left it at home.

Race

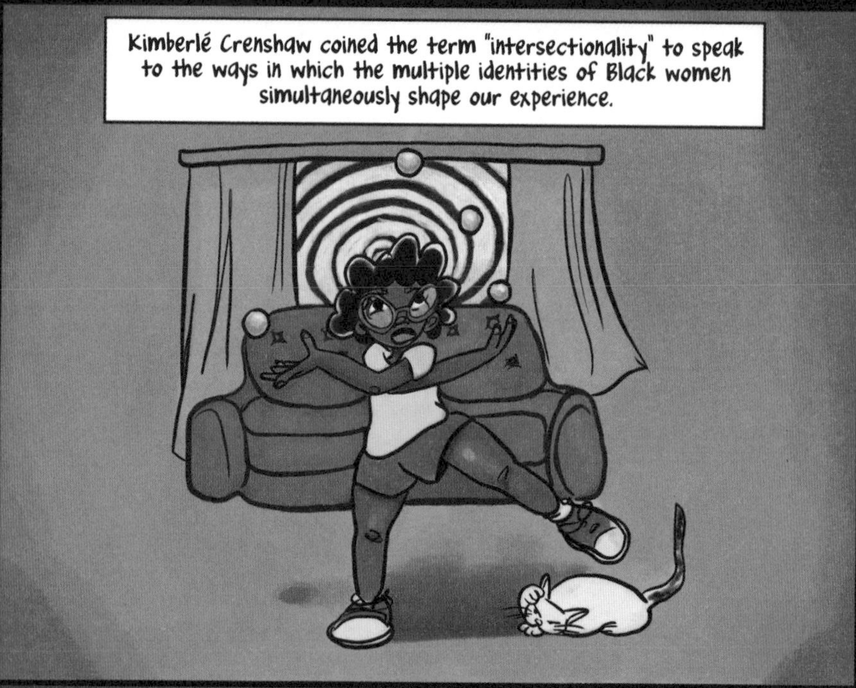
Kimberlé Crenshaw coined the term "intersectionality" to speak to the ways in which the multiple identities of Black women simultaneously shape our experience.

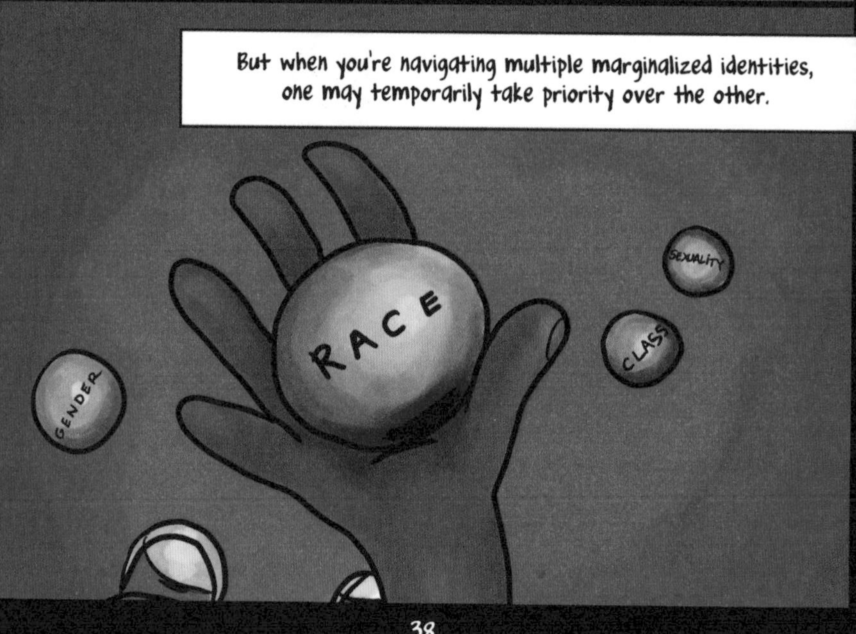
But when you're navigating multiple marginalized identities, one may temporarily take priority over the other.
SEXUALITY
RACE
CLASS
GENDER

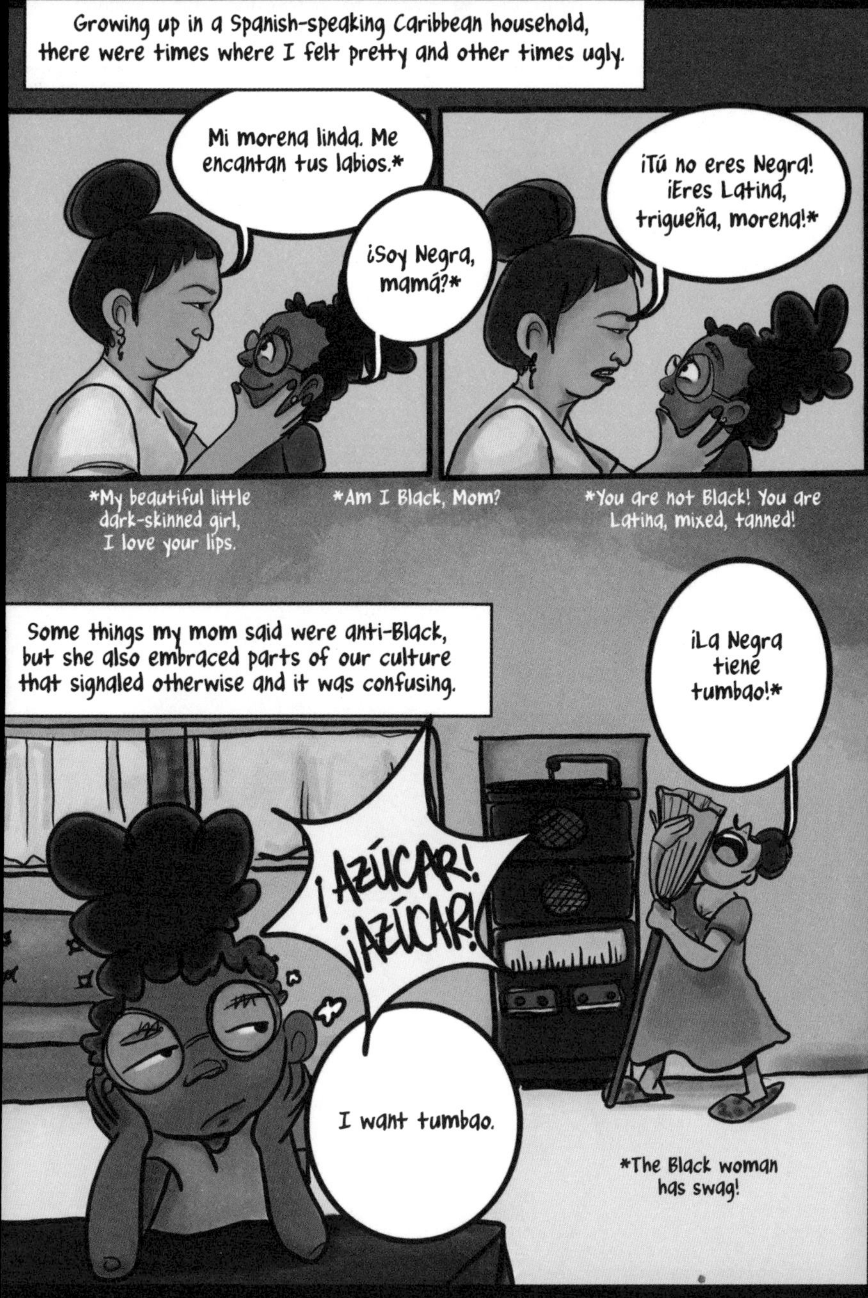
Growing up in a Spanish-speaking Caribbean household, there were times where I felt pretty and other times ugly.
Mi morena linda. Me encantan tus labios.*
¿Soy Negra, mamá?*
¡Tú no eres Negra! ¡Eres Latina, trigueña, morena!*
*My beautiful little dark-skinned girl, I love your lips.
*Am I Black, Mom?
*You are not Black! You are Latina, mixed, tanned!
Some things my mom said were anti-Black, but she also embraced parts of our culture that signaled otherwise and it was confusing.
¡La Negra tiene tumbao!*
¡AZÚCAR! ¡AZÚCAR!
I want tumbao.
*The Black woman has swag!

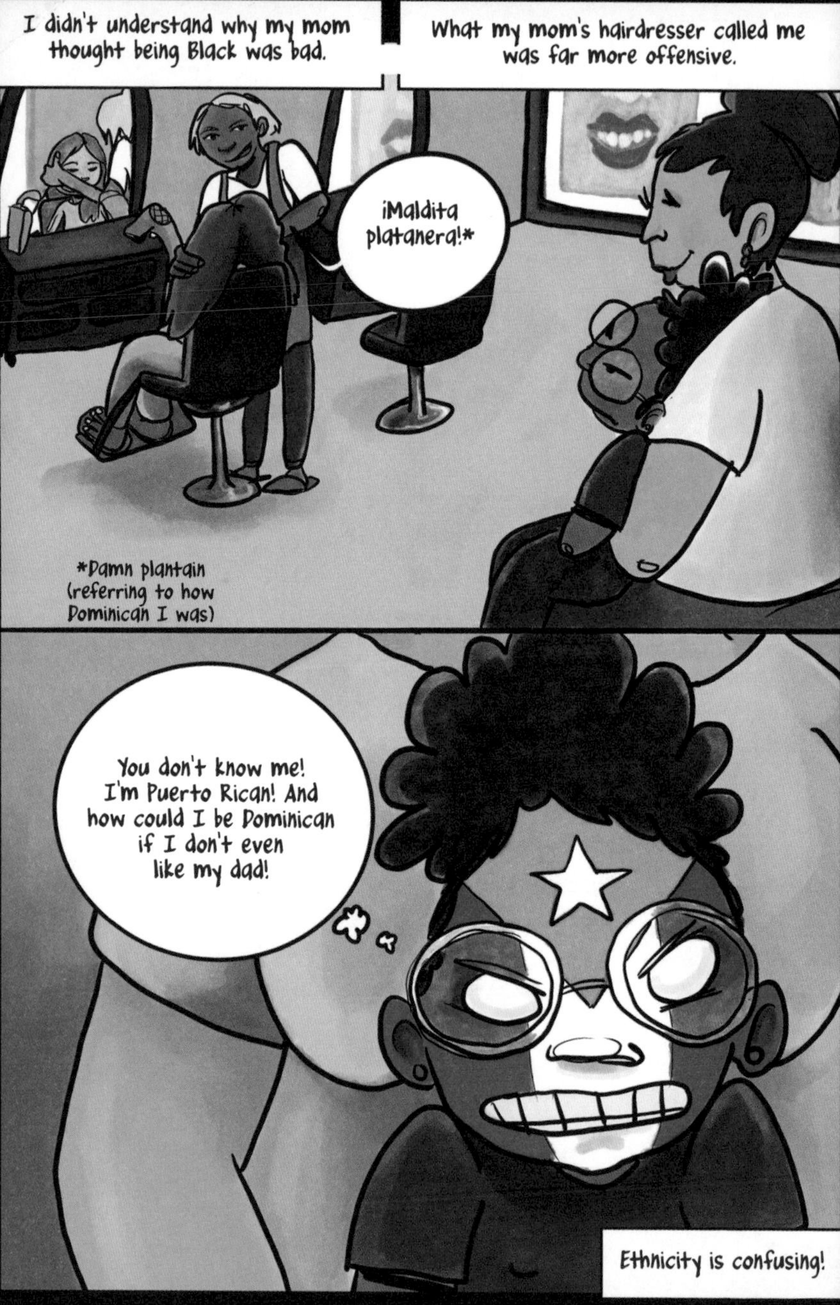
I didn't understand why my mom thought being Black was bad.
What my mom's hairdresser called me was far more offensive.
¡Maldita platanera!*
*Damn plantain (referring to how Dominican I was)
You don't know me! I'm Puerto Rican! And how could I be Dominican if I don't even like my dad!
Ethnicity is confusing!

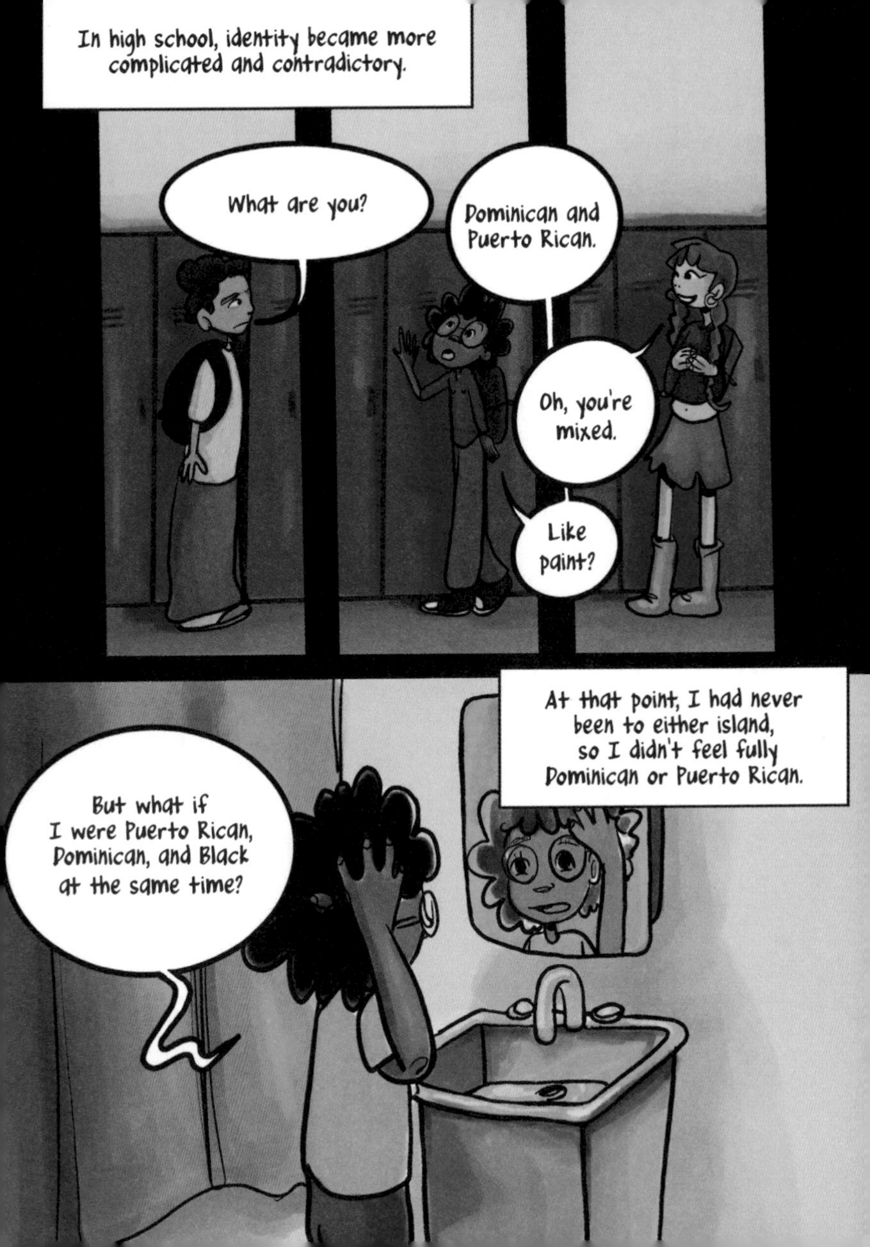
In high school, identity became more complicated and contradictory.
What are you?
Dominican and Puerto Rican.
Oh, you're mixed.
Like paint?
At that point, I had never been to either island, so I didn't feel fully Dominican or Puerto Rican.
But what if I were Puerto Rican, Dominican, and Black at the same time?

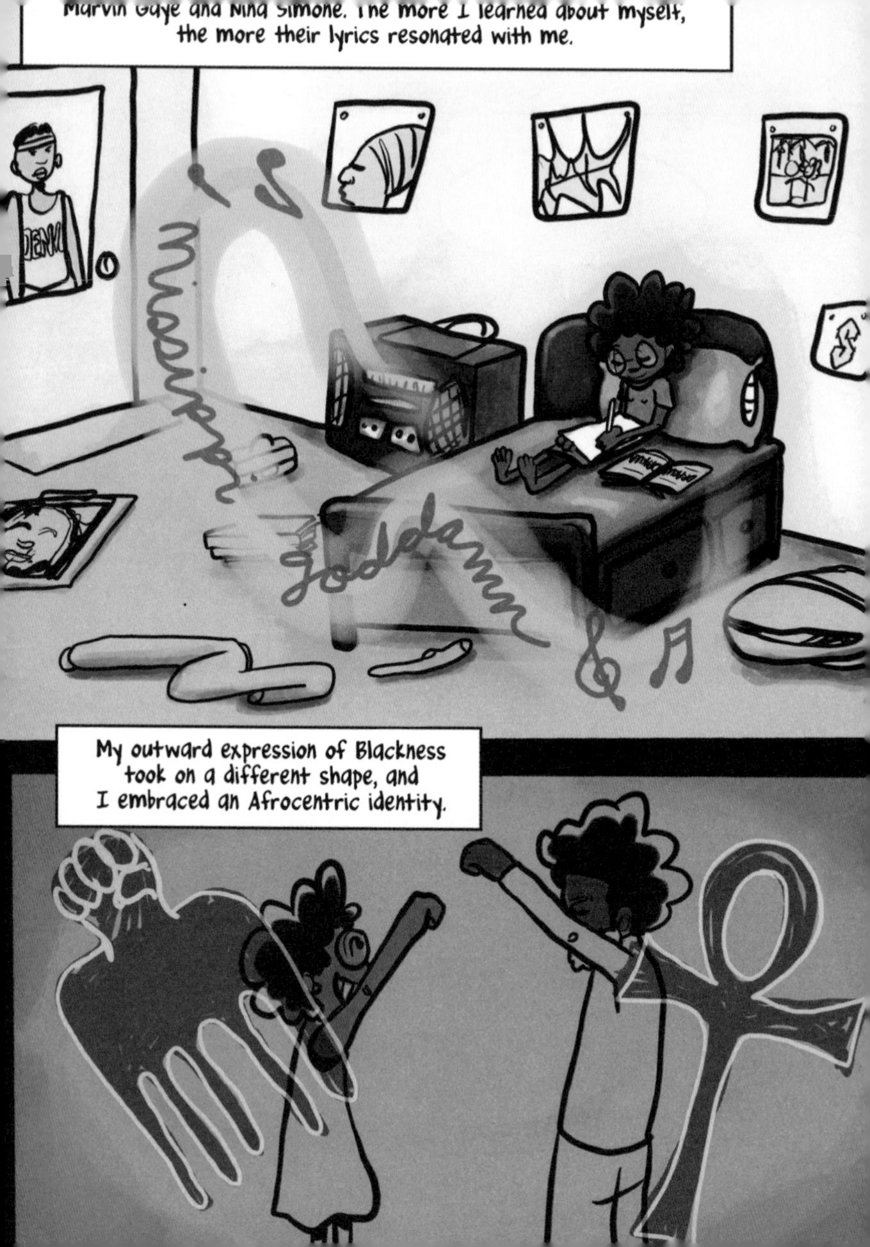
Marvin Gaye and Nina Simone. The more I learned about myself, the more their lyrics resonated with me.
My outward expression of Blackness took on a different shape, and I embraced an Afrocentric identity.

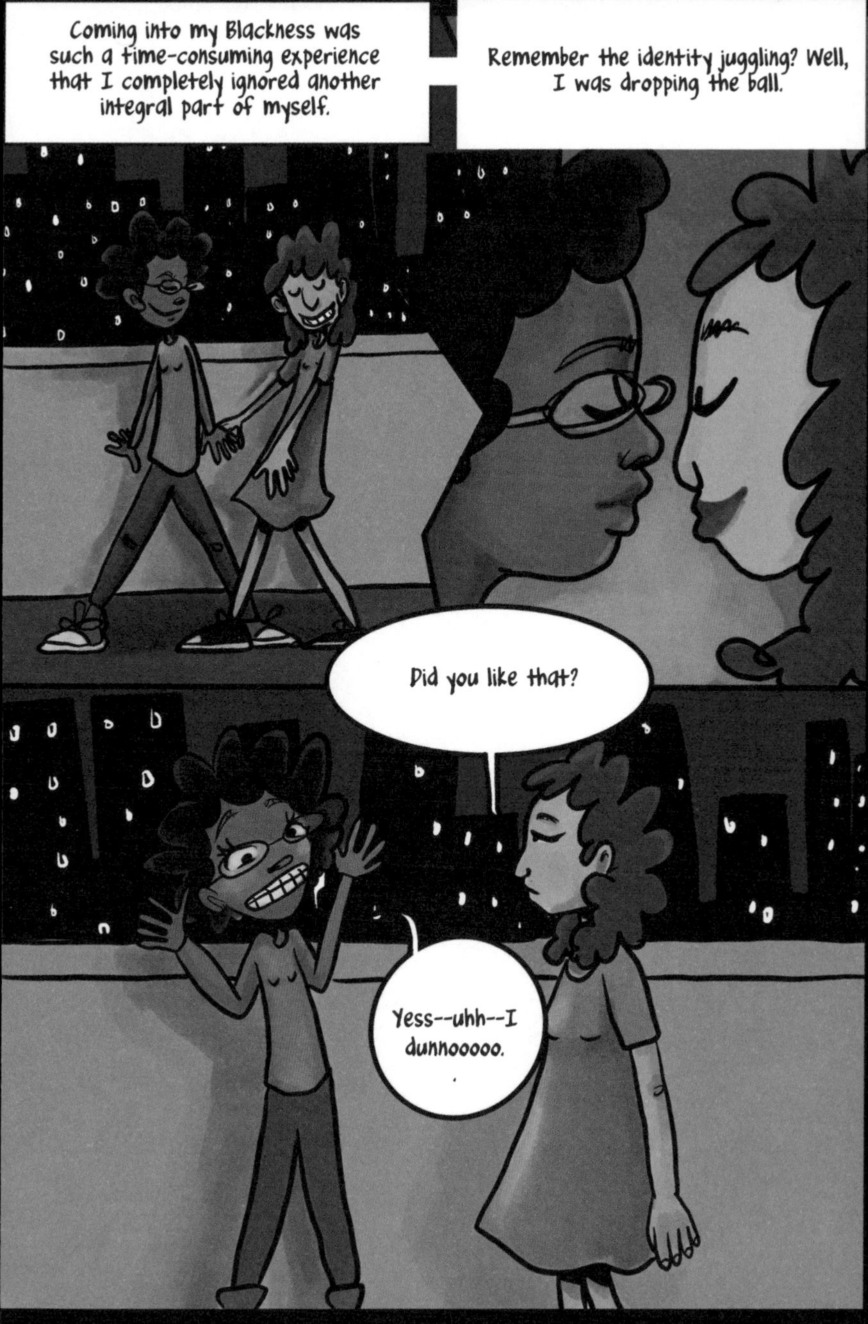

Coming into my Blackness was such a time-consuming experience that I completely ignored another integral part of myself.
Remember the identity juggling? Well, I was dropping the ball.
Did you like that?
Yess--uhh--I dunnooooo.

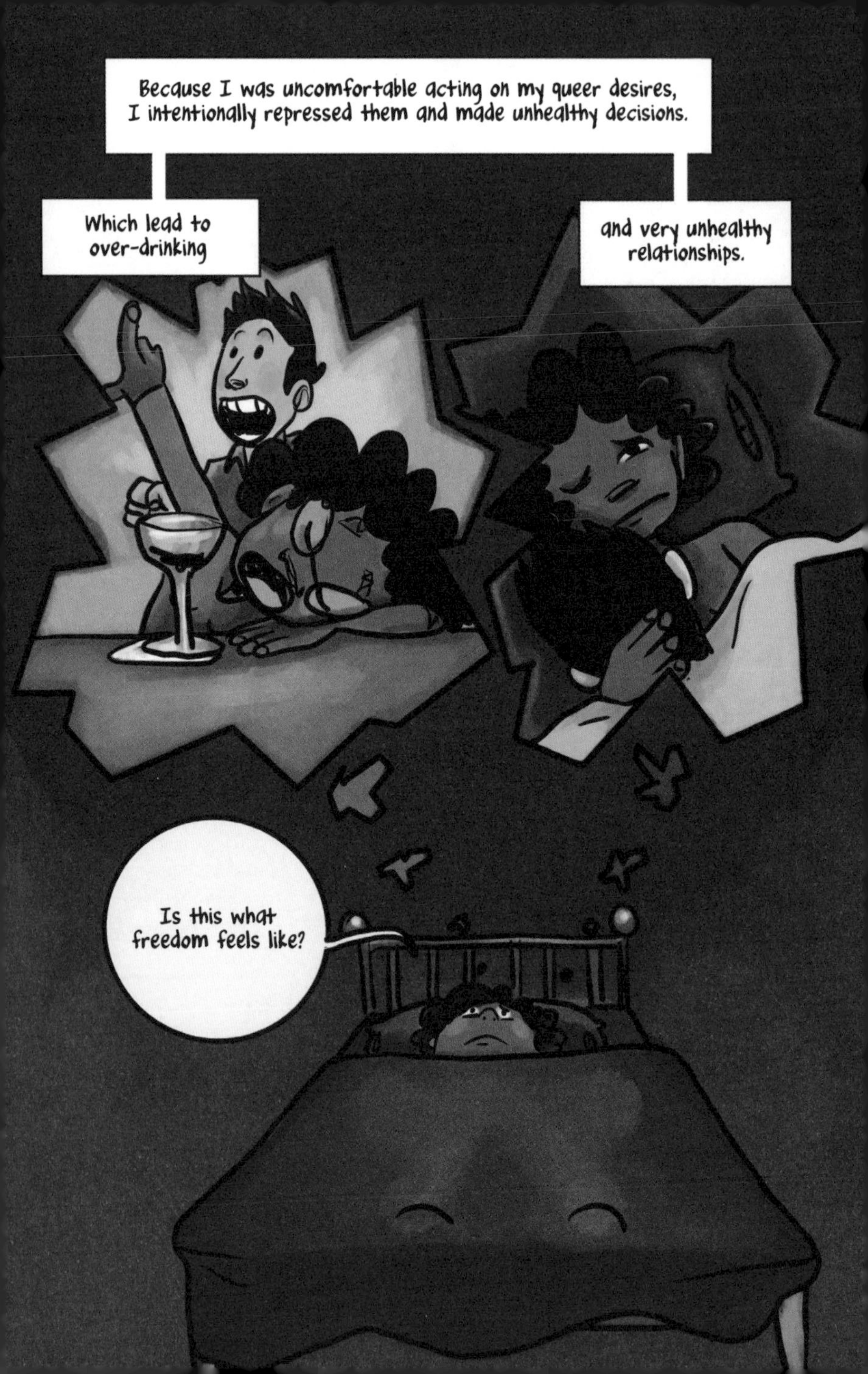
Because I was uncomfortable acting on my queer desires, I intentionally repressed them and made unhealthy decisions.
Which lead to over-drinking
and very unhealthy relationships.
Is this what freedom feels like?

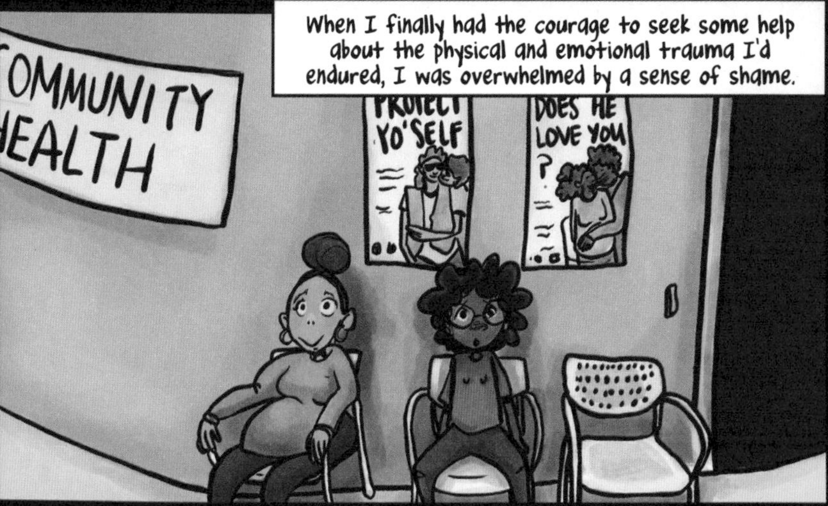
When I finally had the courage to seek some help about the physical and emotional trauma I'd endured, I was overwhelmed by a sense of shame.
COMMUNITY HEALTH
PROTECT YO'SELF
DOES HE LOVE YOU ?

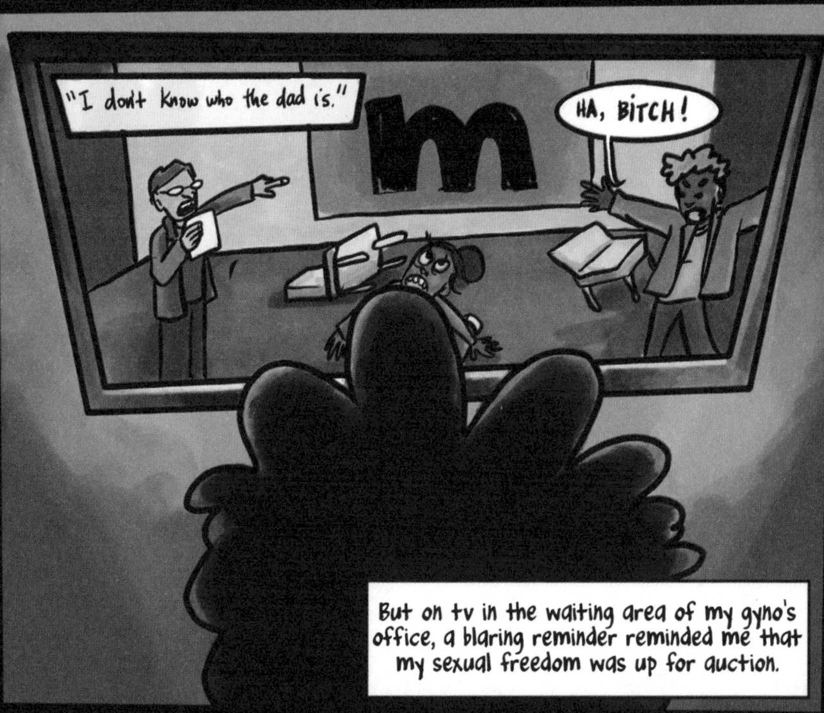
"I don't know who the dad is."
HA, BITCH!
But on tv in the waiting area of my gyno's office, a blaring reminder reminded me that my sexual freedom was up for auction.

IS THIS FREEDOM?
ANTI BIOTICS
You're nasty
THOT
Foolish
SHAME
You fell for that?
Lazy

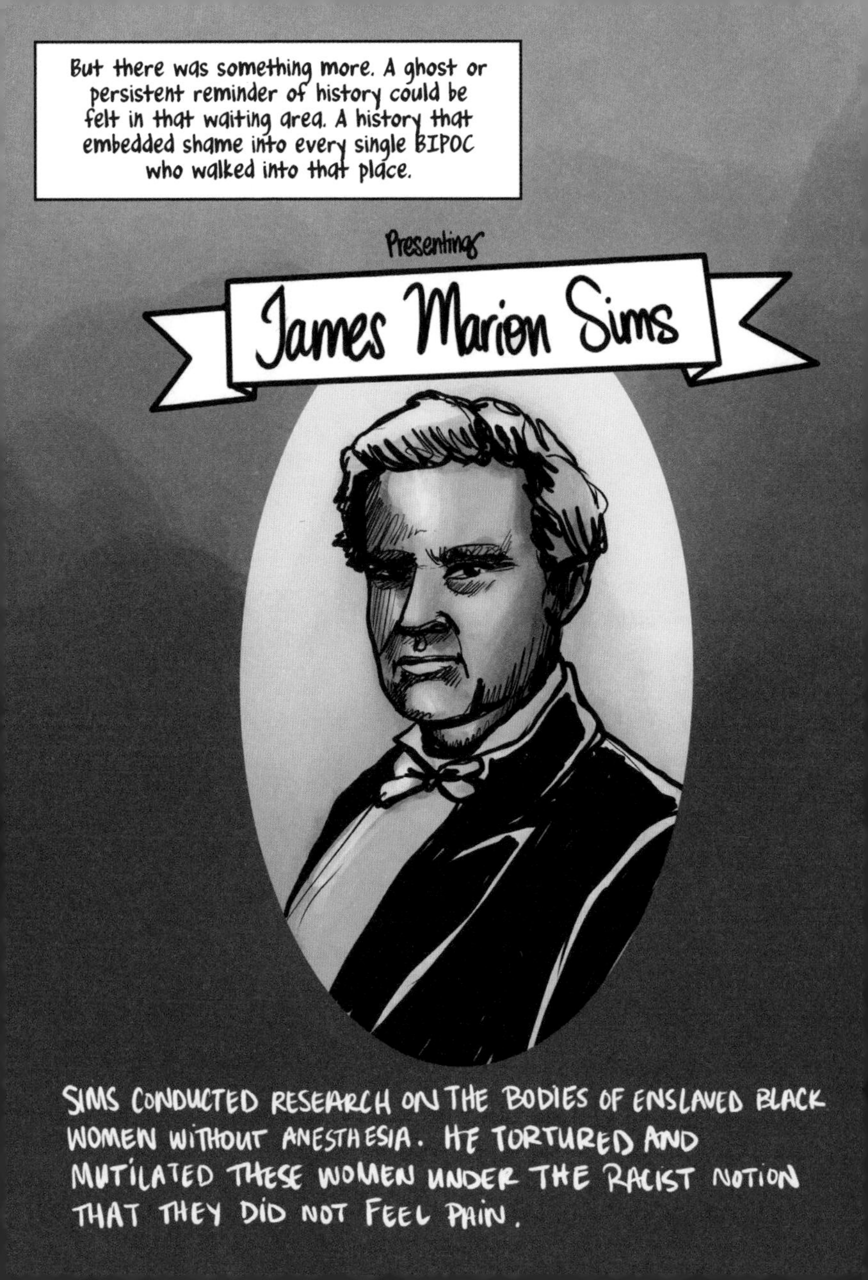
But there was something more. A ghost or persistent reminder of history could be felt in that waiting area. A history that embedded shame into every single BIPOC who walked into that place.
Presenting:
James Marion Sims
SIMS CONDUCTED RESEARCH ON THE BODIES OF ENSLAVED BLACK WOMEN WITHOUT ANESTHESIA. HE TORTURED AND MUTILATED THESE WOMEN UNDER THE RACIST NOTION THAT THEY DID NOT FEEL PAIN.

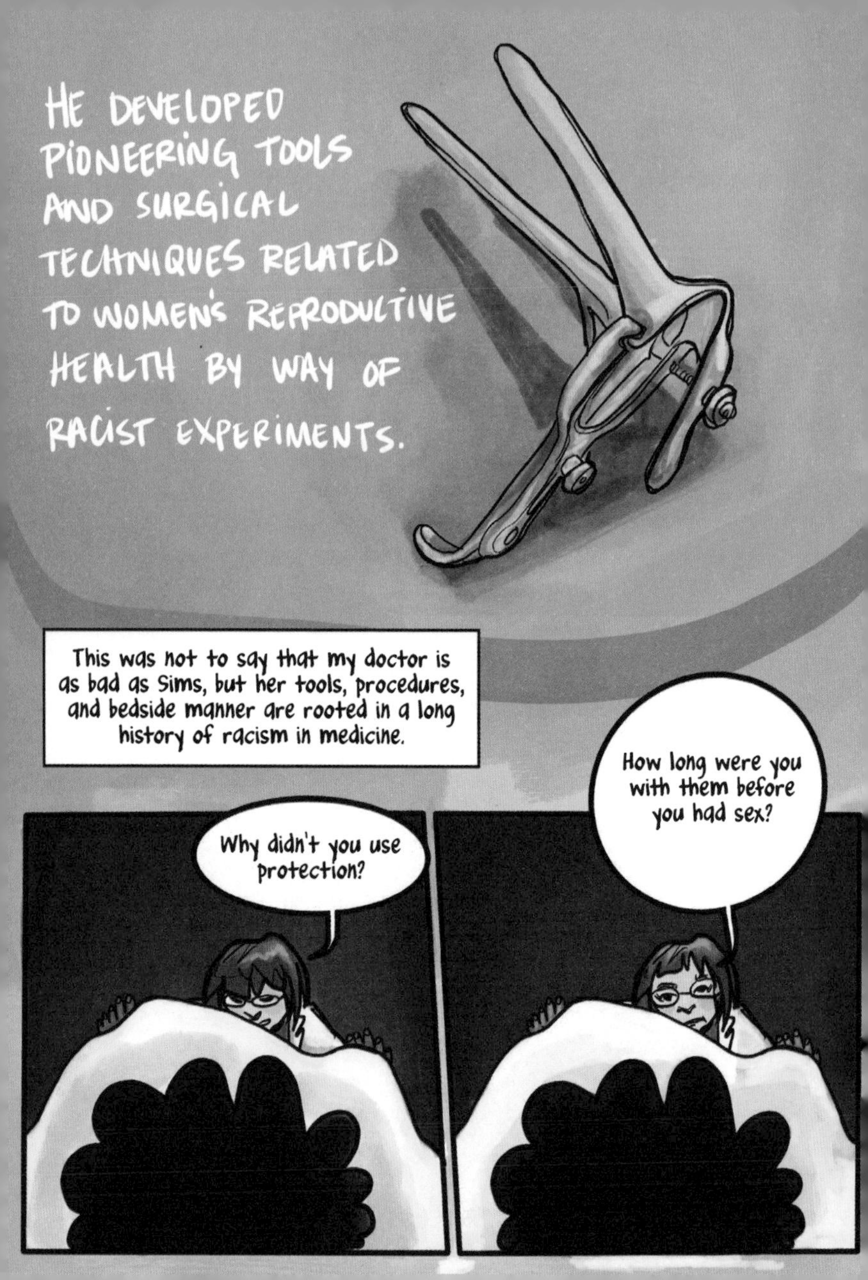

HE DEVELOPED PIONEERING TOOLS AND SURGICAL TECHNIQUES RELATED TO WOMEN'S REPRODUCTIVE HEALTH BY WAY OF RACIST EXPERIMENTS.

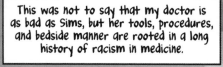

This was not to say that my doctor is as bad as Sims, but her tools, procedures, and bedside manner are rooted in a long history of racism in medicine.

Why didn't you use protection?

How long were you with them before you had sex?

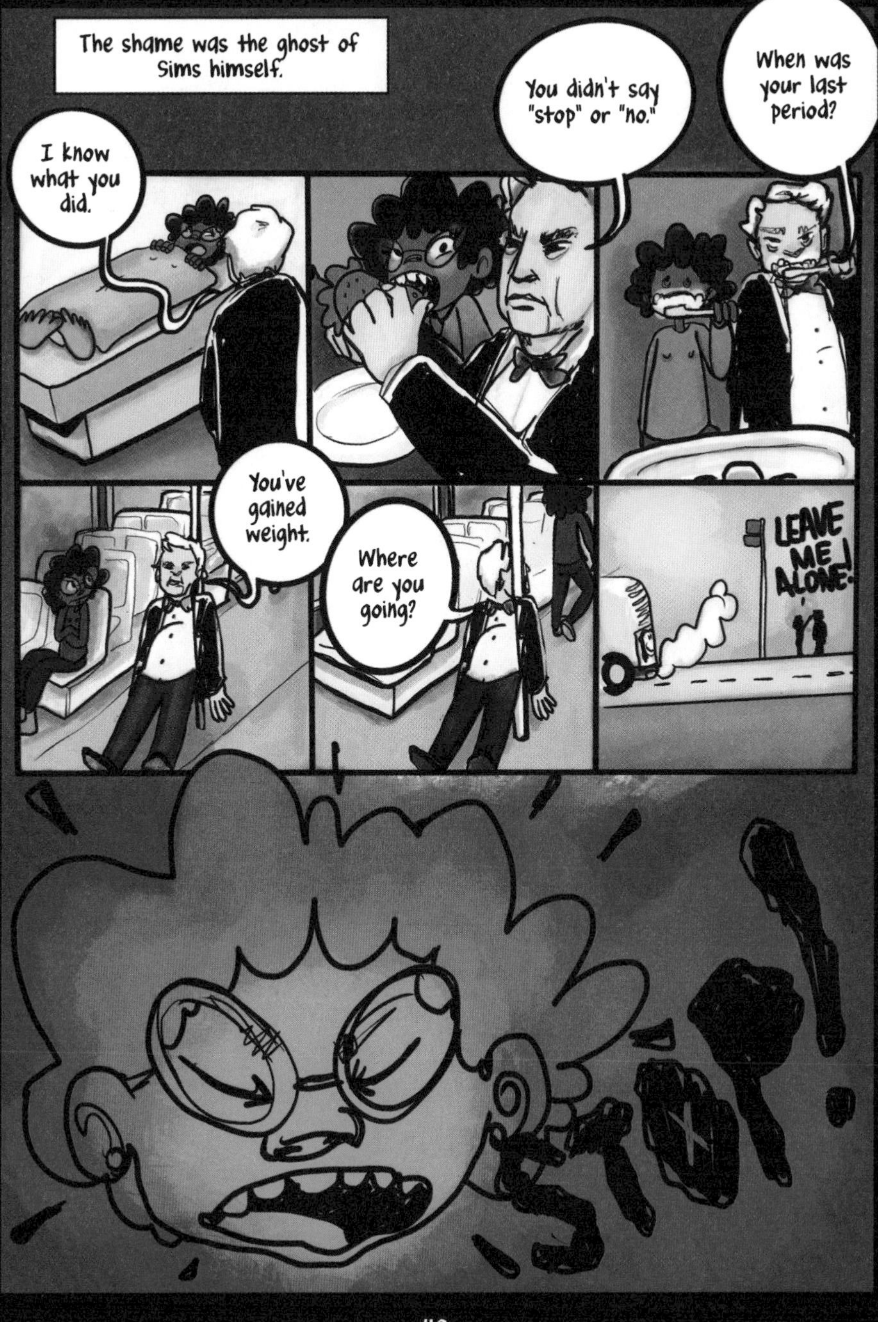
The shame was the ghost of Sims himself.
I know what you did.
You didn't say "stop" or "no."
When was your last period?
You've gained weight.
Where are you going?
LEAVE ME ALONE!

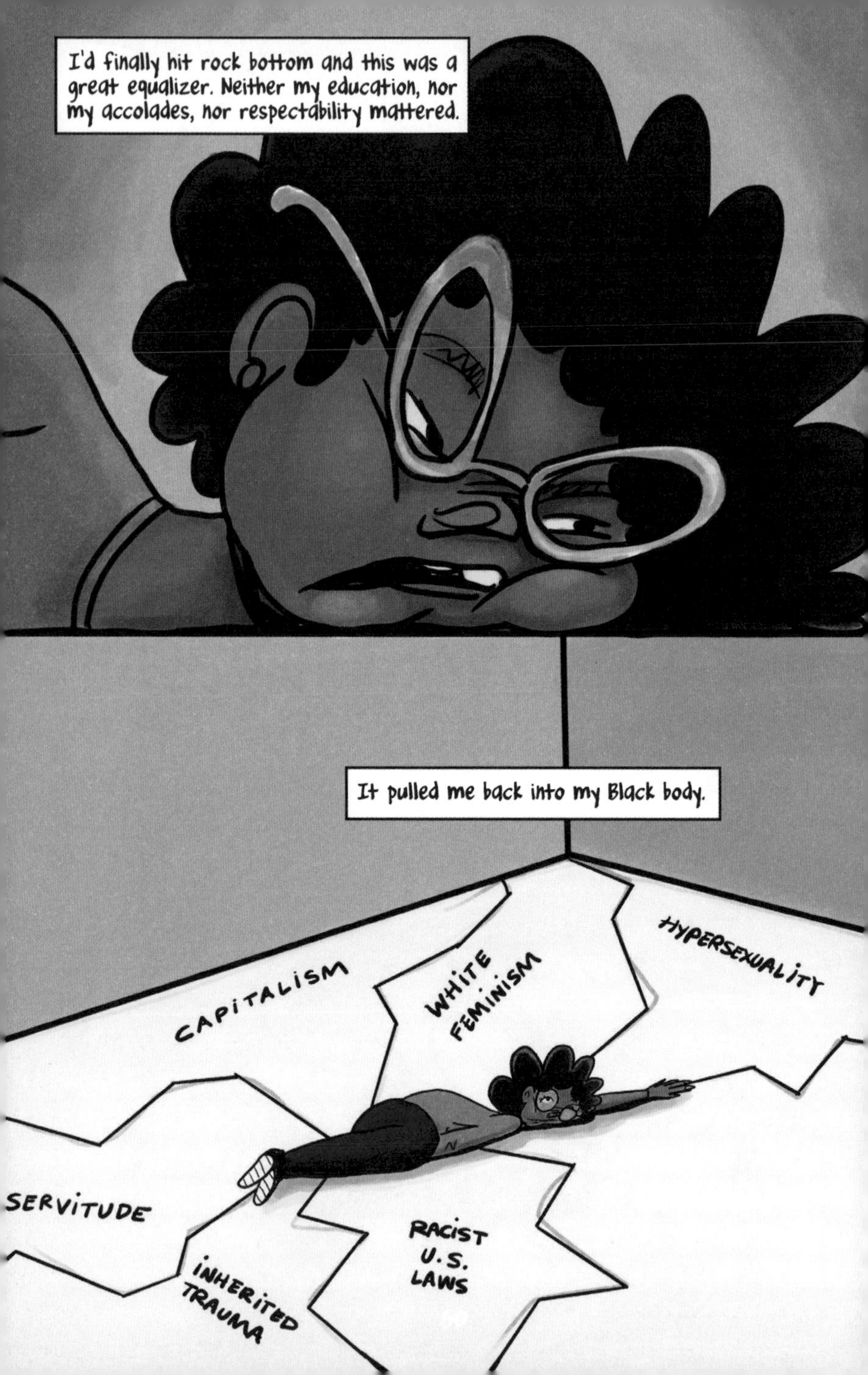
I'd finally hit rock bottom and this was a great equalizer. Neither my education, nor my accolades, nor respectability mattered.
It pulled me back into my Black body.
CAPITALISM
WHITE FEMINISM
HYPERSEXUALITY
SERVITUDE
RACIST U.S. LAWS
INHERITED TRAUMA

How did I become a statistic? Dr. Melissa Harris-Perry, a sociologist, author, and professor has a theory on this.

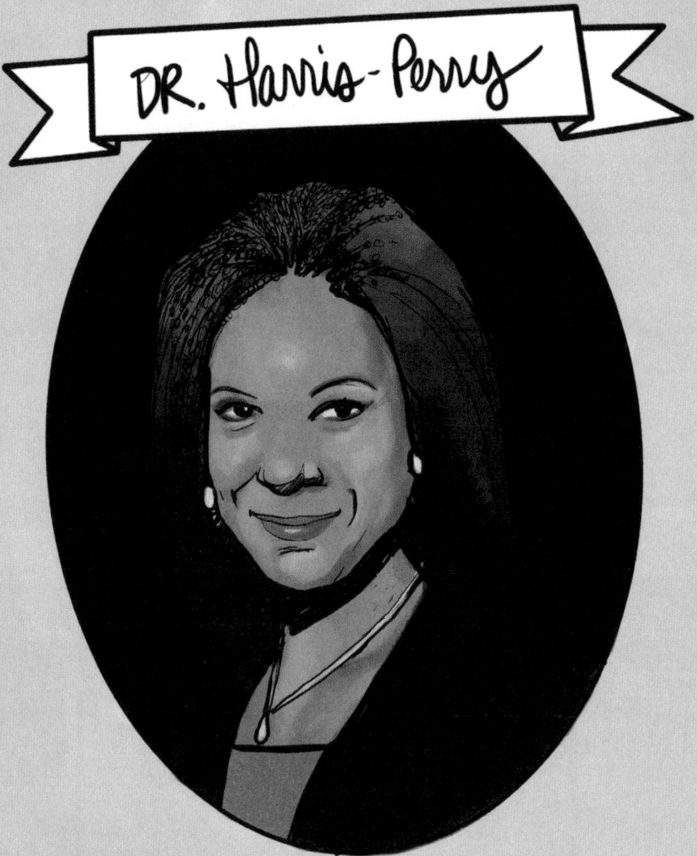
DR. Harris-Perry

HER RESEARCH SUGGESTS THAT RACIAL SHAME IS A DIRECT CAUSE OF THE STATISTICS DISPROPORTIONATELY AFFECTING BLACK WOMEN.

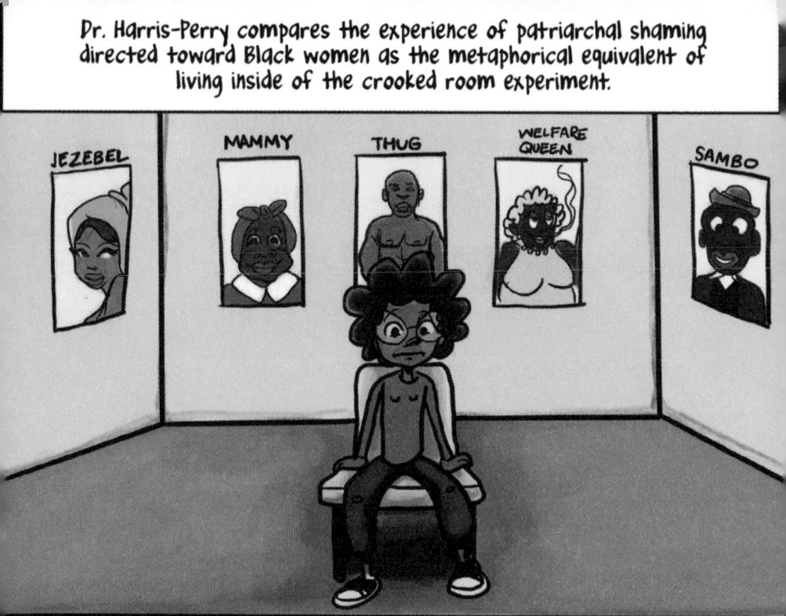
Dr. Harris-Perry compares the experience of patriarchal shaming directed toward Black women as the metaphorical equivalent of living inside of the crooked room experiment.
JEZEBEL
MAMMY
THUG
WELFARE QUEEN
SAMBO

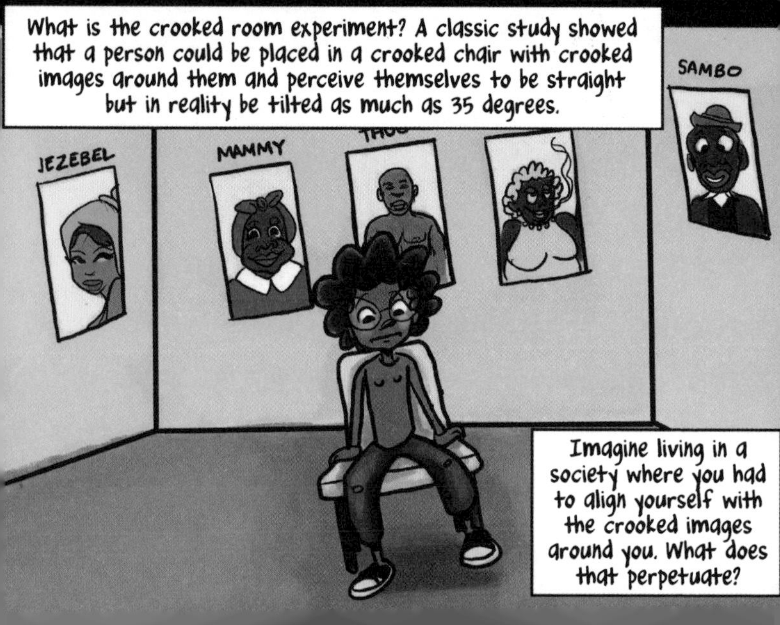
What is the crooked room experiment? A classic study showed that a person could be placed in a crooked chair with crooked images around them and perceive themselves to be straight but in reality be tilted as much as 35 degrees.
SAMBO
JEZEBEL
MAMMY
WELFARE QUEEN
Imagine living in a society where you had to align yourself with the crooked images around you. What does that perpetuate?

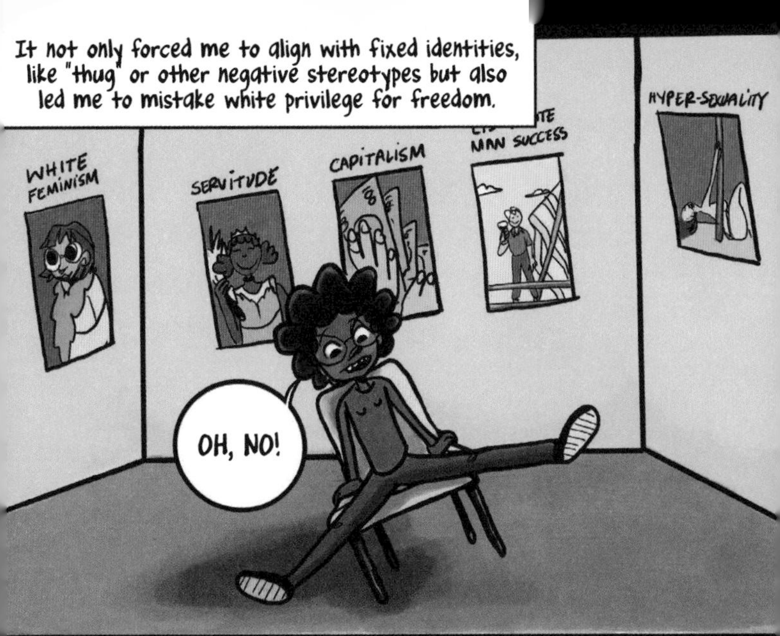
It not only forced me to align with fixed identities, like "thug" or other negative stereotypes but also led me to mistake white privilege for freedom.
WHITE FEMINISM
SERVITUDE
CAPITALISM
MAN SUCCESS
HYPER-SEXUALITY
OH, NO!

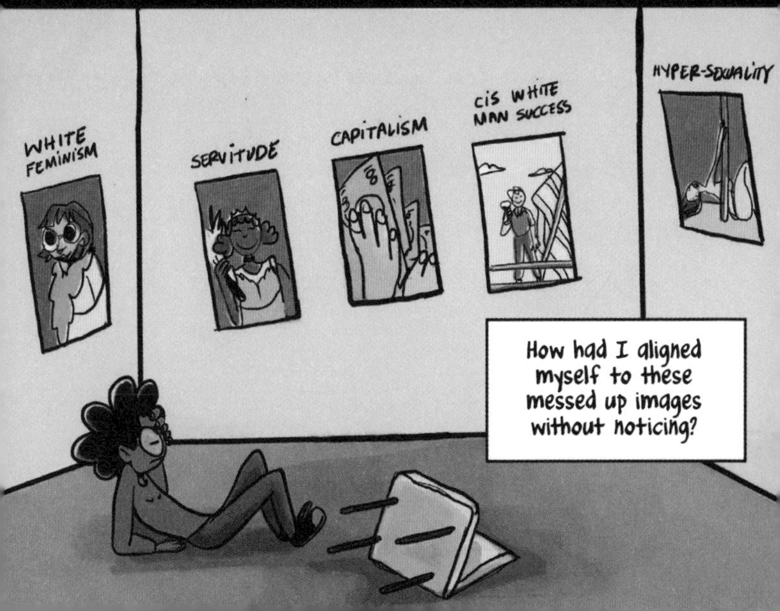
WHITE FEMINISM
SERVITUDE
CAPITALISM
CIS WHITE MAN SUCCESS
HYPER-SEXUALITY
How had I aligned myself to these messed up images without noticing?

See, this is much larger than one individual racist, like Sims.
This is about long-lasting effects on laws, education, and policies.
Professor Harris-Perry makes this connection in U.S. history.

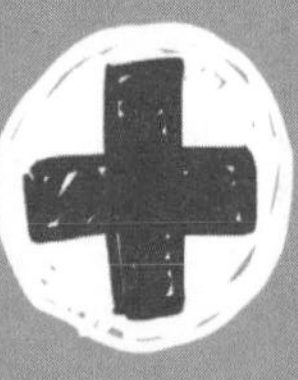

INDIVIDUALS WHO DON'T CONFORM TO WHITE SOCIAL NORMS ARE MORE EXPOSED TO CHRONIC SHAMING AND SHAMING UNDERMINES HEALTH.

SO IMAGINE A TIME IN U.S. HISTORY WHEN WE LEGALIZED SHAME. IT'S CALLED

THE JIM CROW LAWS

(ENFORCED LEGALLY UNTIL 1965)

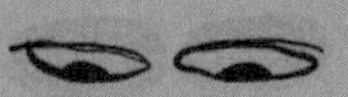

LOWERED GAZE

WHITES → / COLORED ← FORCED SEPARATION

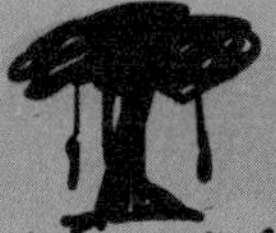

LYNCHING

And continued racism throughout U.S. history painted Black women in a particular light

- BLAMED FOR SOCIAL DISORDER DURING THE GREAT MIGRATION
- LABELED MATRIARCHS BY MOYNIHAN
- DESCRIBED AS "WELFARE QUEENS" BY REAGAN

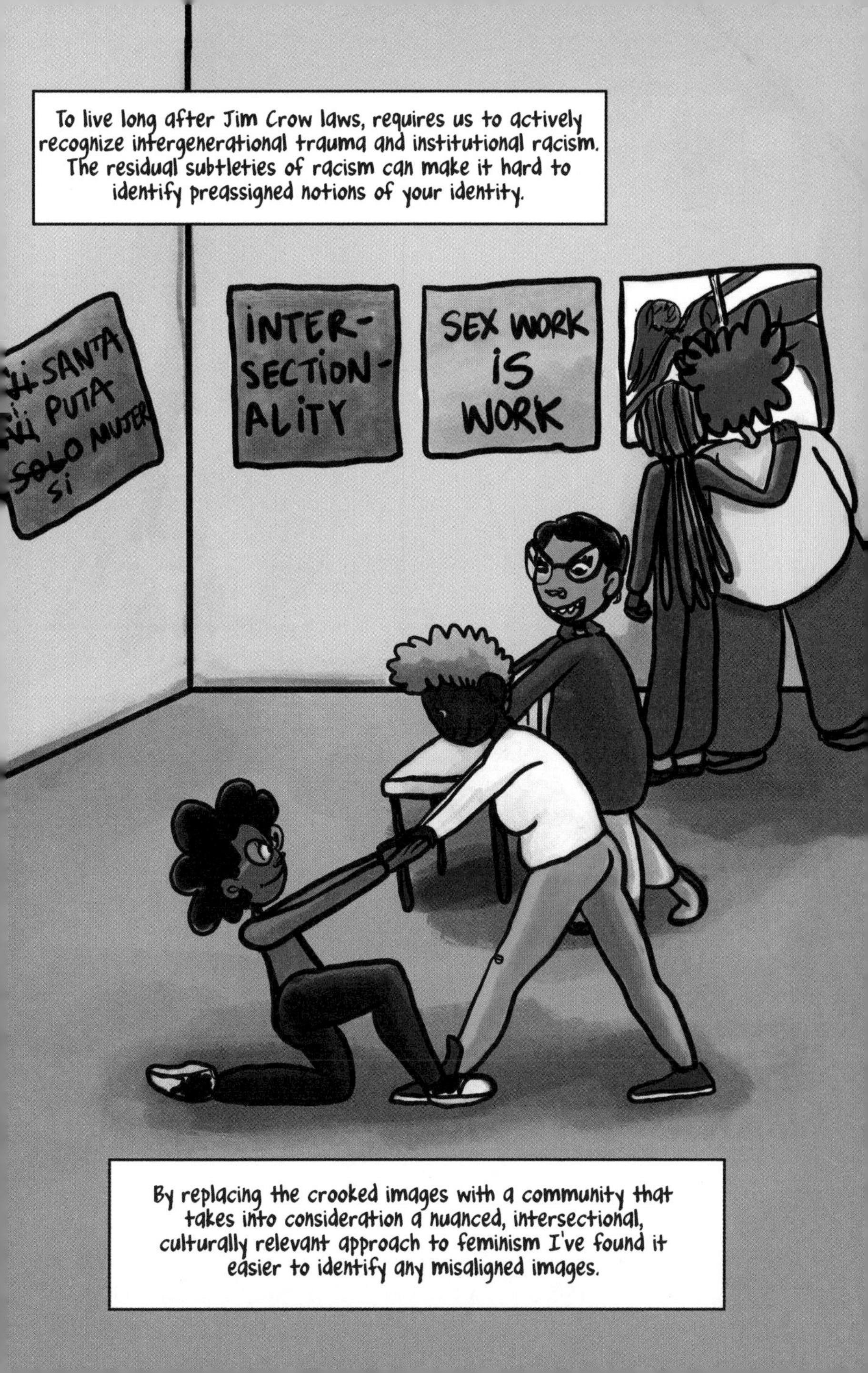
To live long after Jim Crow laws, requires us to actively recognize intergenerational trauma and institutional racism. The residual subtleties of racism can make it hard to identify preassigned notions of your identity.
SANTA
PUTA
SOLO MUJER
SI
INTER-SECTION-ALITY
SEX WORK IS WORK
By replacing the crooked images with a community that takes into consideration a nuanced, intersectional, culturally relevant approach to feminism I've found it easier to identify any misaligned images.

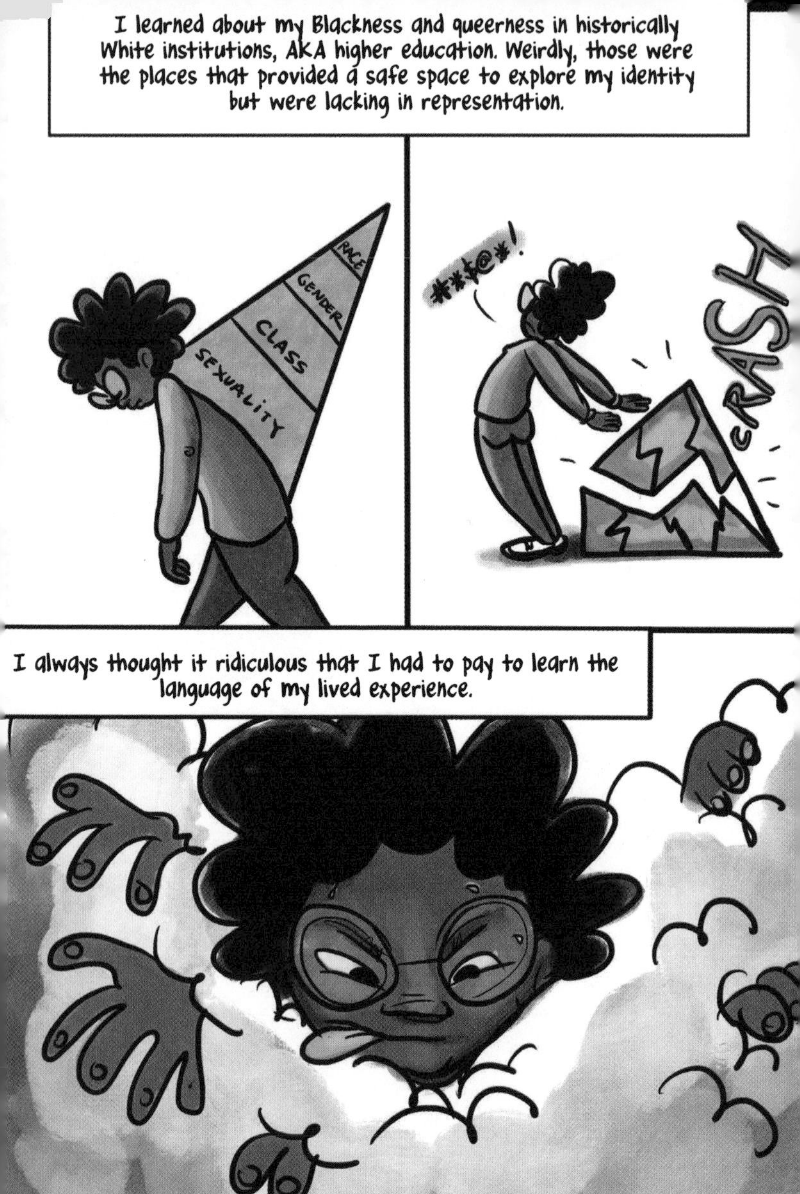
I learned about my Blackness and queerness in historically White institutions, AKA higher education. Weirdly, those were the places that provided a safe space to explore my identity but were lacking in representation.
RACE
GENDER
CLASS
SEXUALITY
**$@*!
CRASH
I always thought it ridiculous that I had to pay to learn the language of my lived experience.

But no matter how or when, as I continuously gather the language I need, it allows me to better arrange how I carry my identities. Instead of a heavy backpack, I choose to wear them as armor.

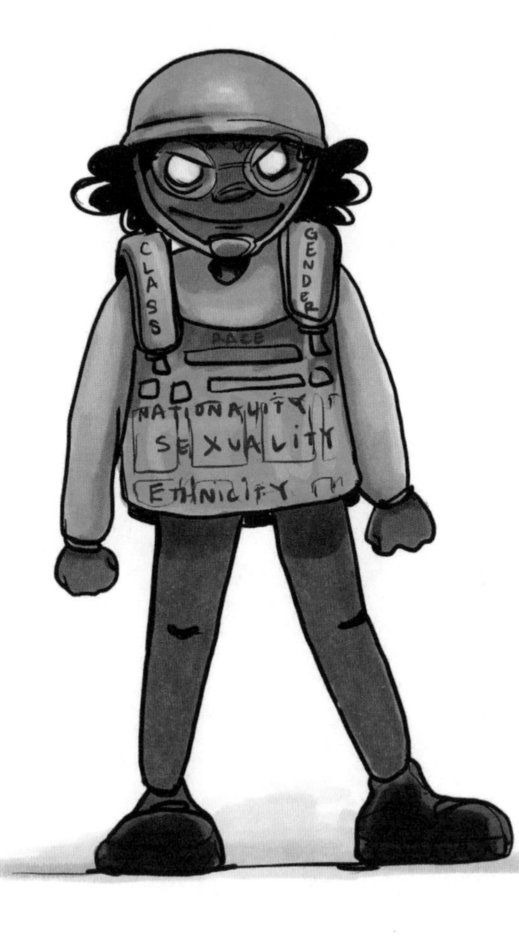
CLASS
GENDER
RACE
NATIONALITY
SEXUALITY
ETHNICITY

5
UNeVentful
coMing Out
Story

Coming out can be stressful, dangerous, and have major consequences. This is the reason why I didn't come out for a long time. But my story, in particular, was not like that. In fact, it was quite uneventful . . .

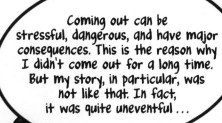

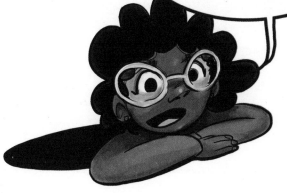

Welcome to The Bronx, NY

The Bronx
Terminal
Market Mall

Applebees —
Mother's Day 2017

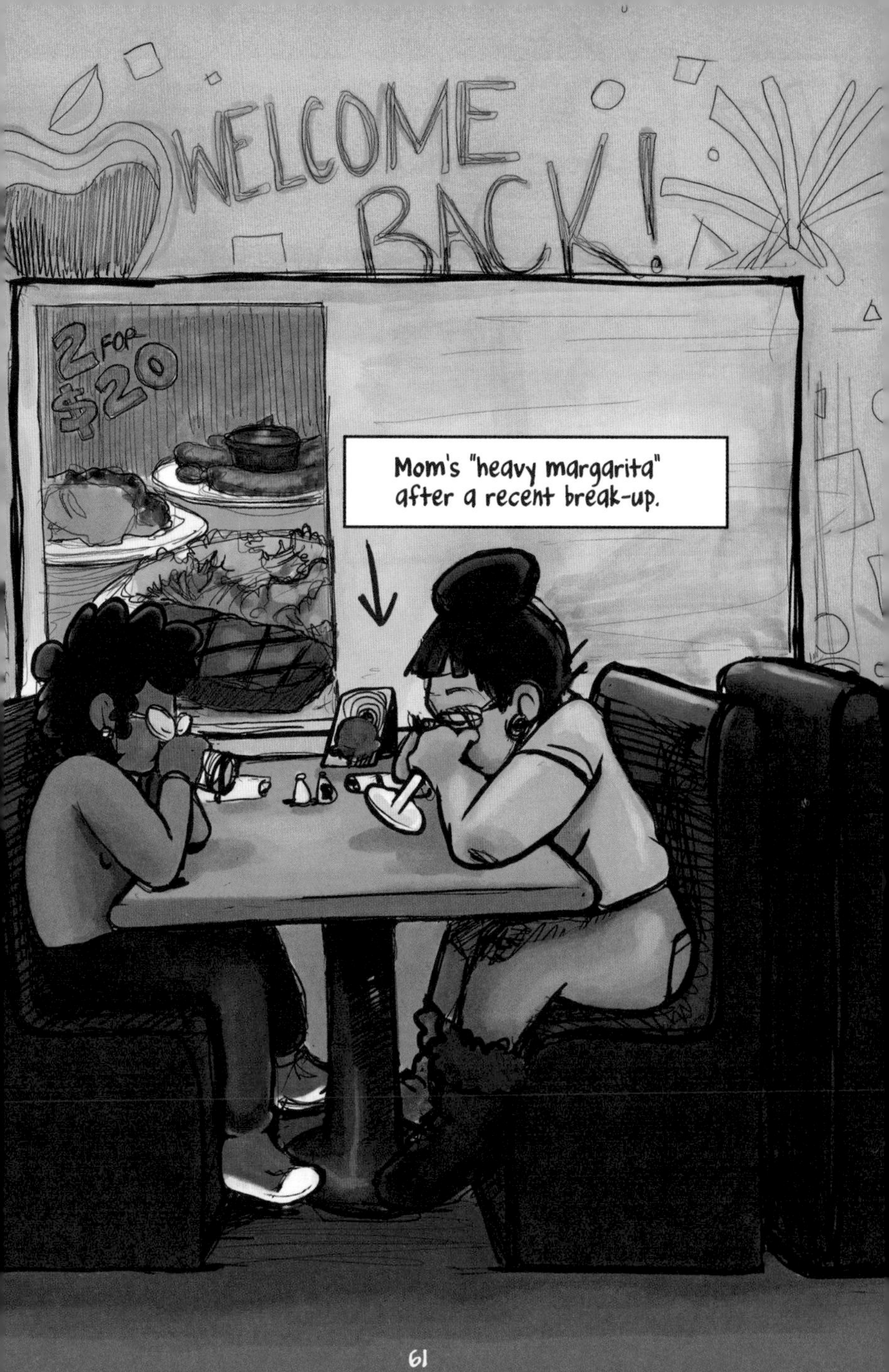
WELCOME BACK!
2 FOR $20
Mom's "heavy margarita" after a recent break-up.

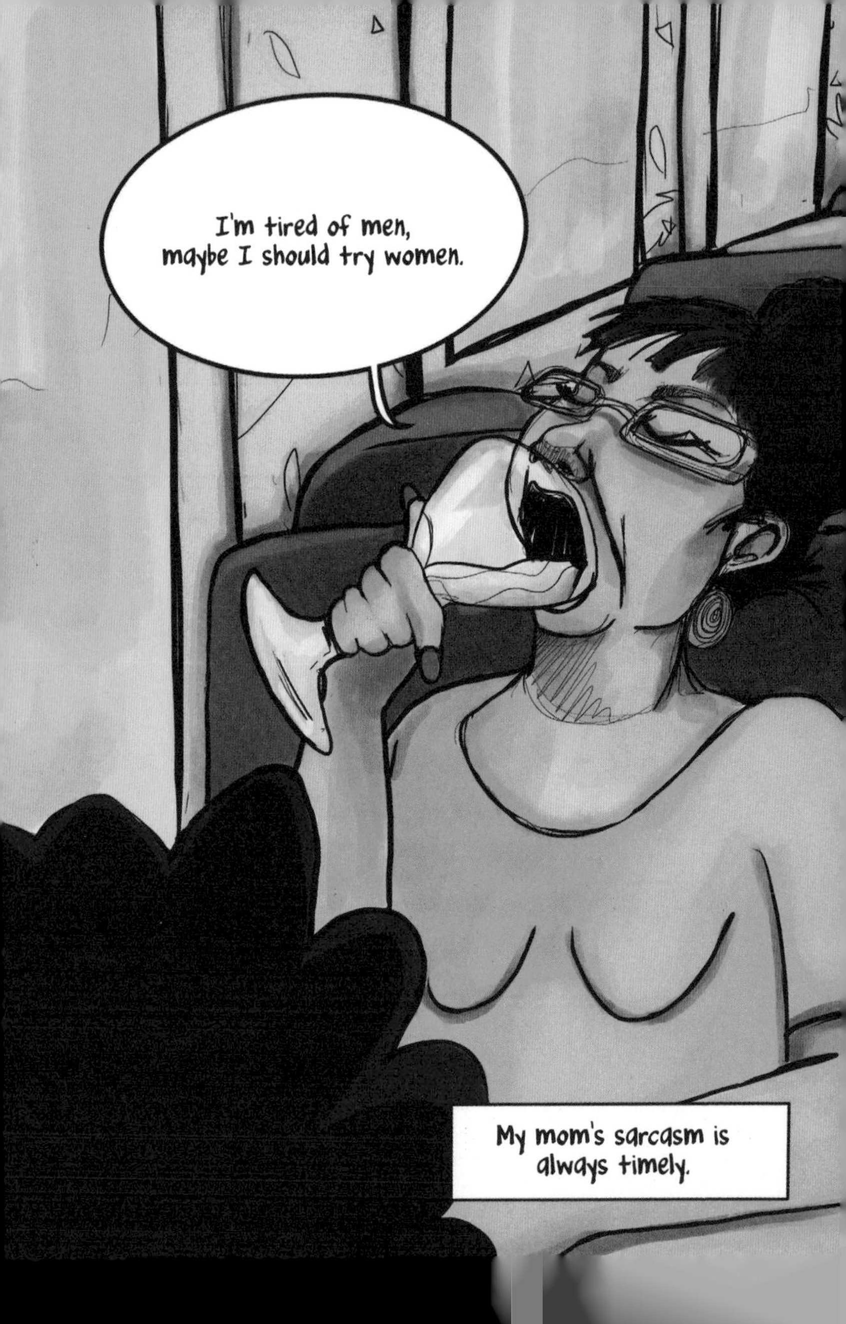
I'm tired of men, maybe I should try women.
My mom's sarcasm is always timely.

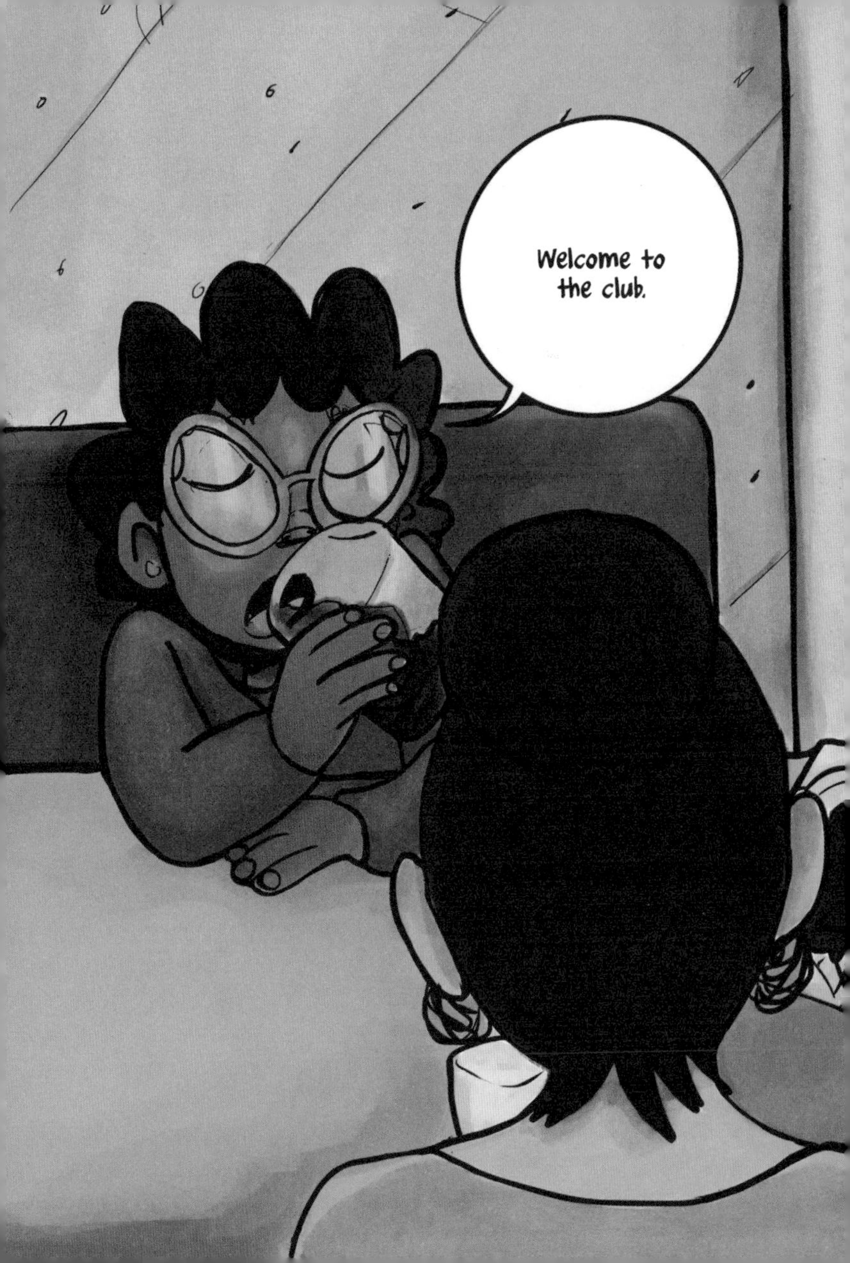
Welcome to the club.

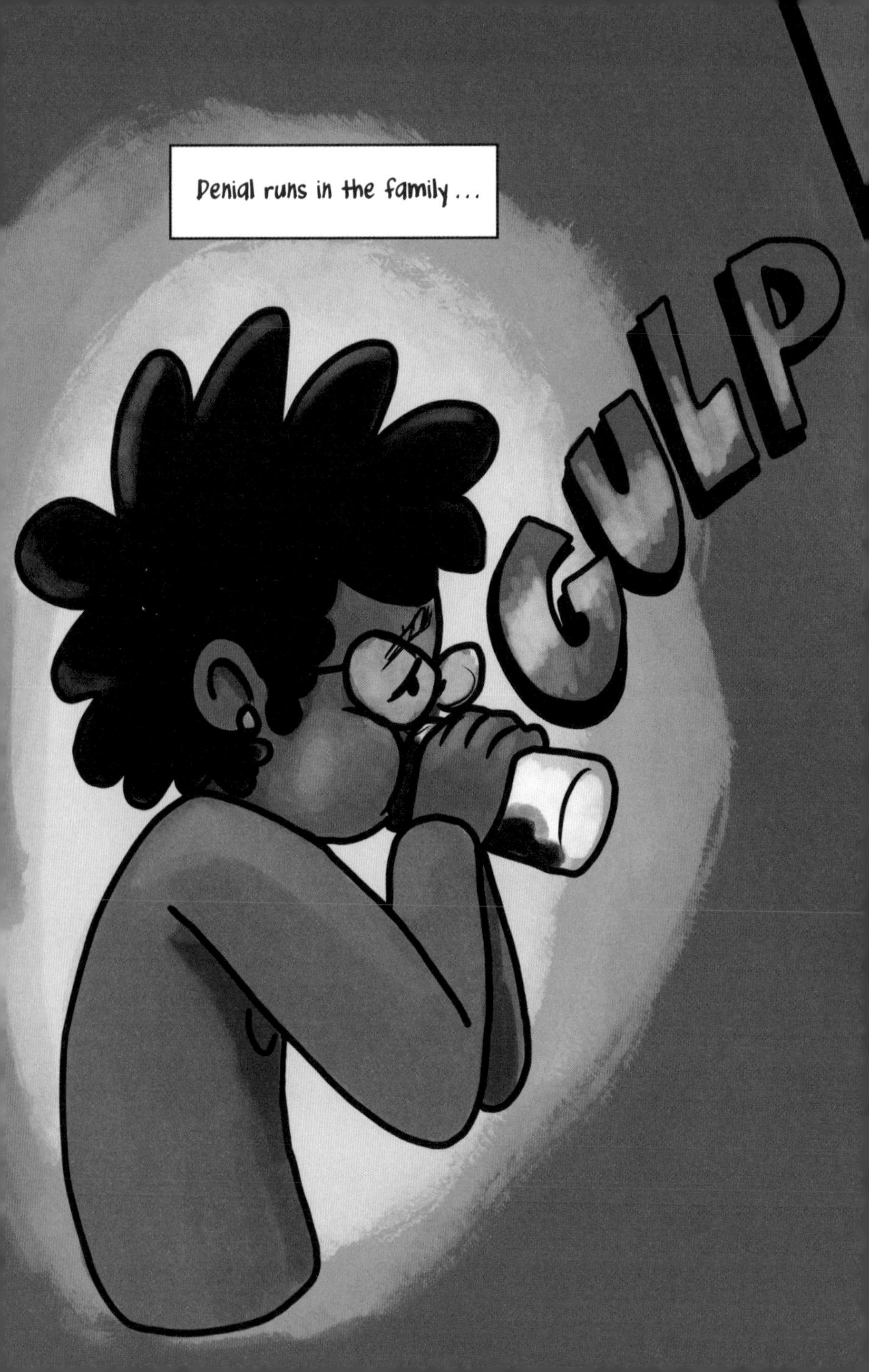
Denial runs in the family...
GULP

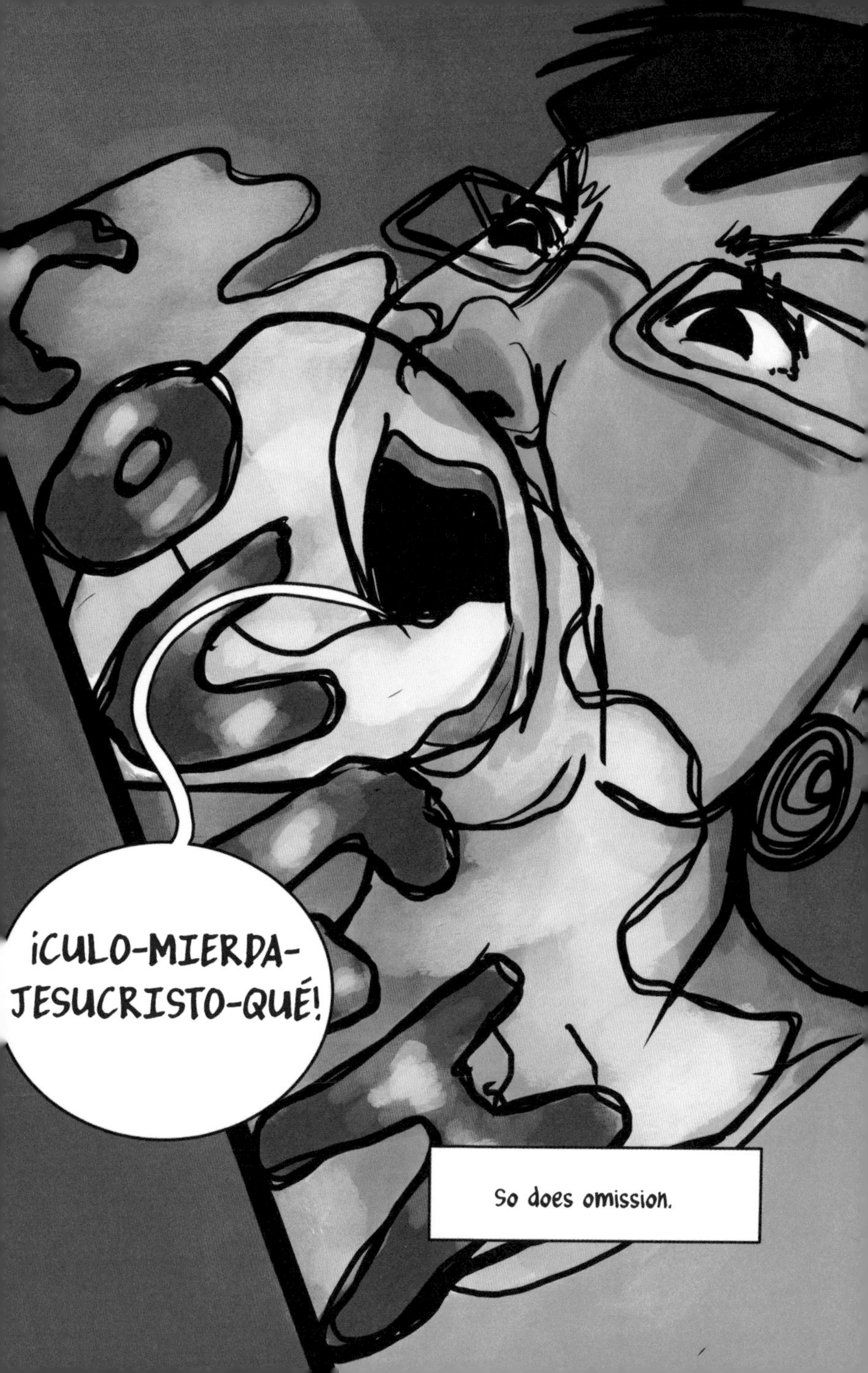
¡CULO-MIERDA-JESUCRISTO-QUÉ!
So does omission.

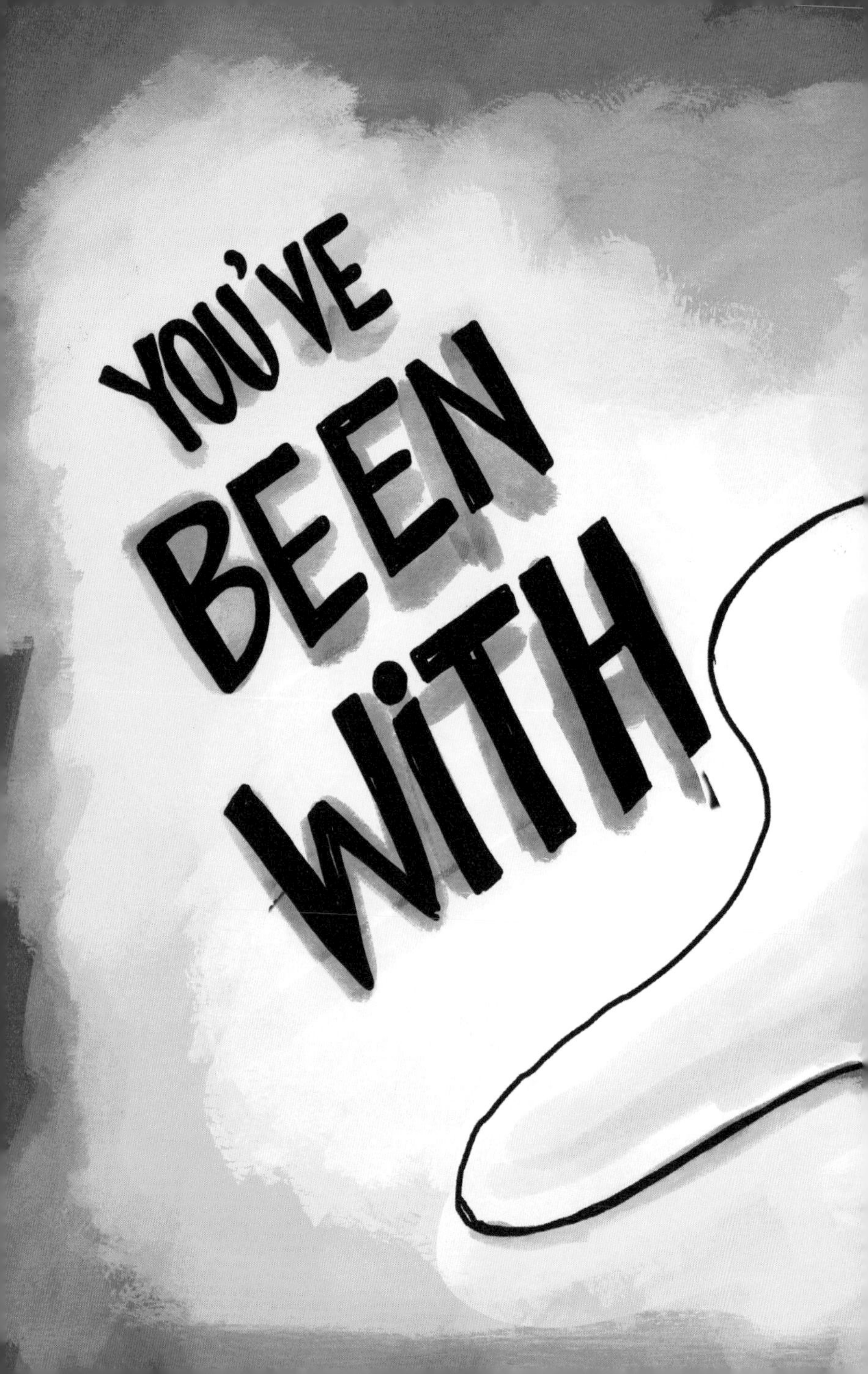
YOU'VE BEEN WITH

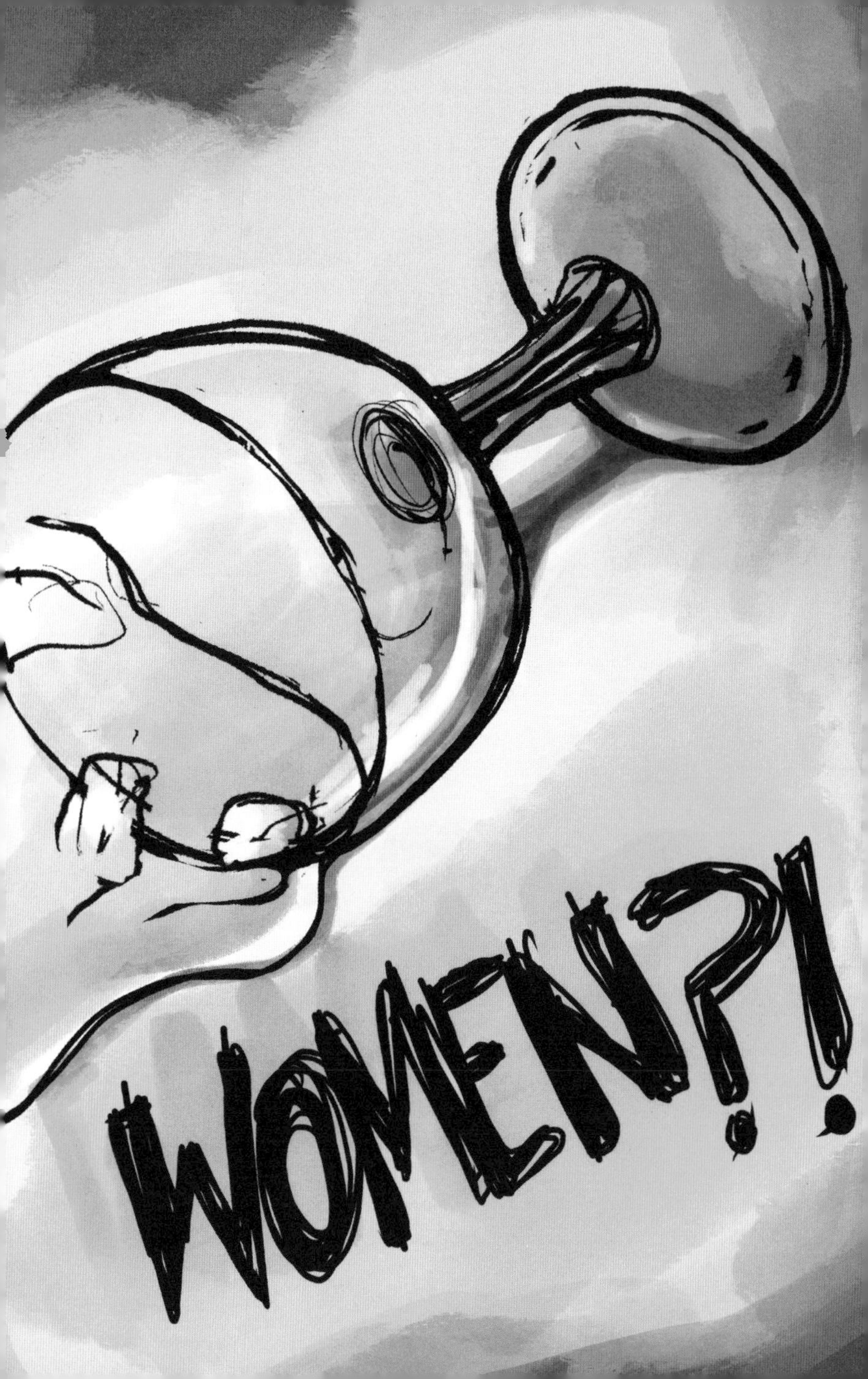
WOMEN?!

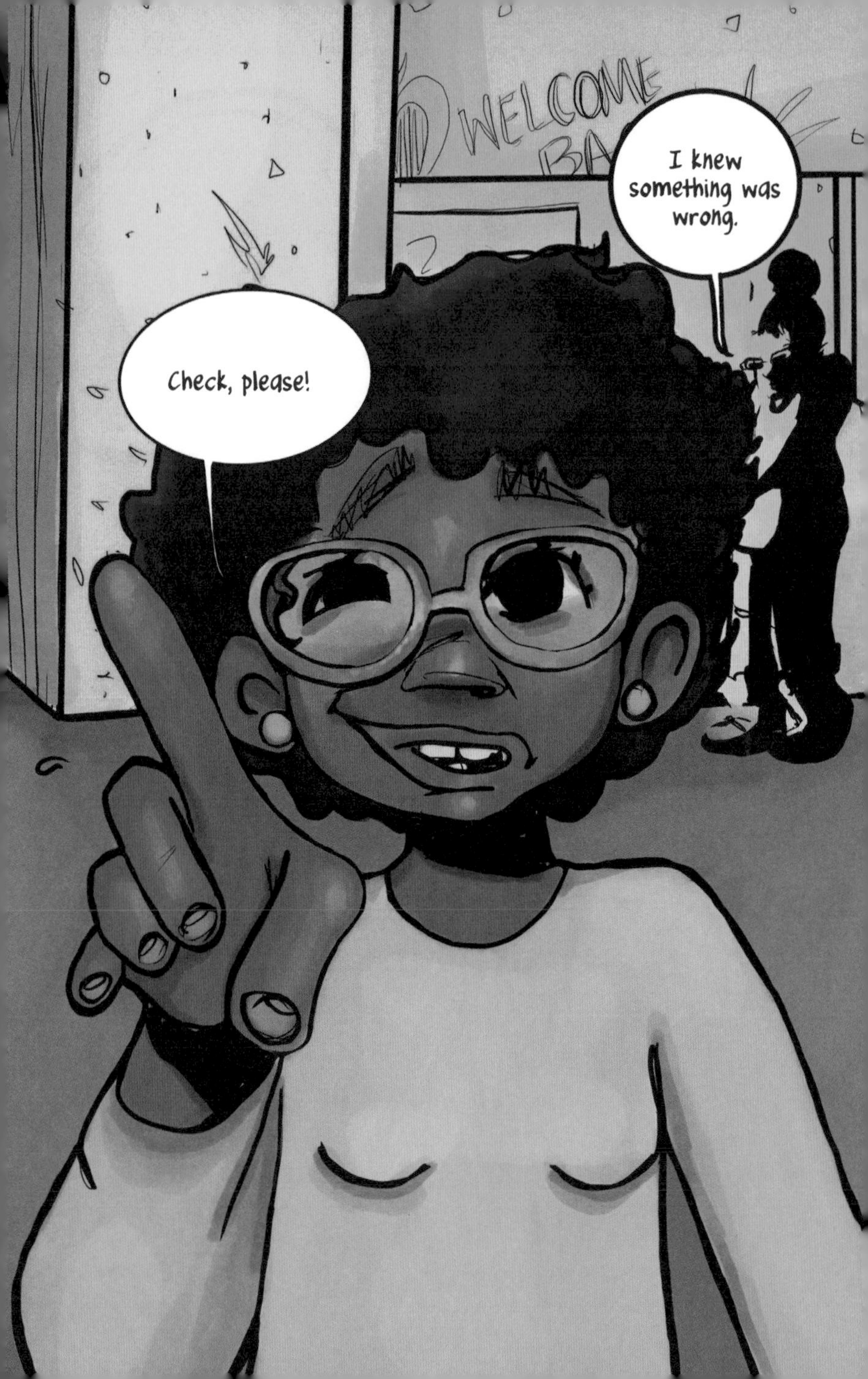
I knew something was wrong.
Check, please!
WELCOME

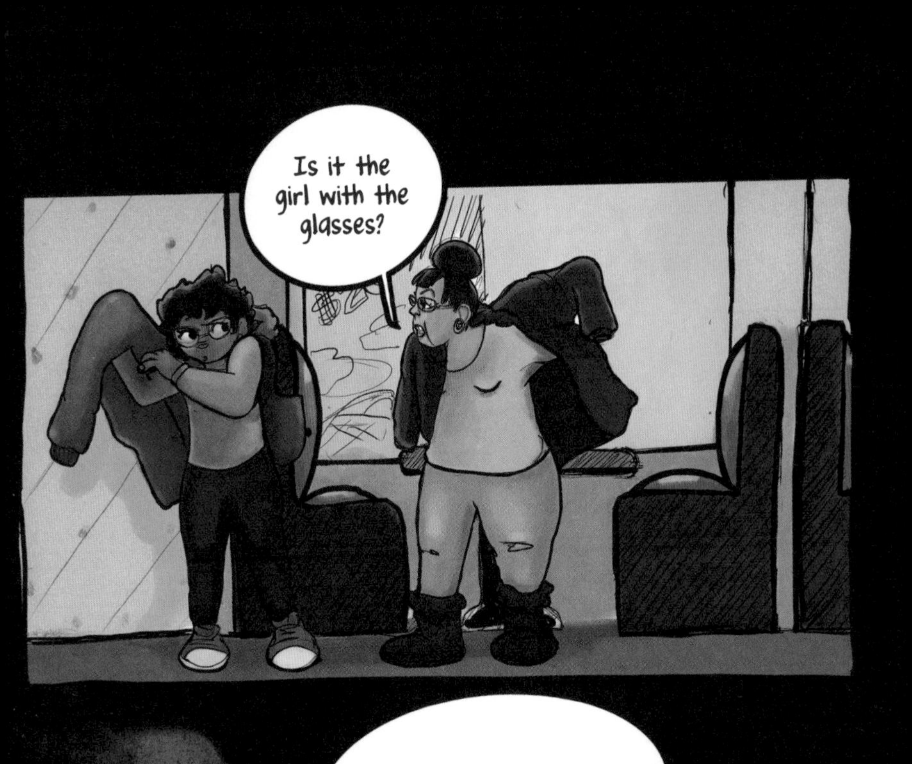
Is it the girl with the glasses?

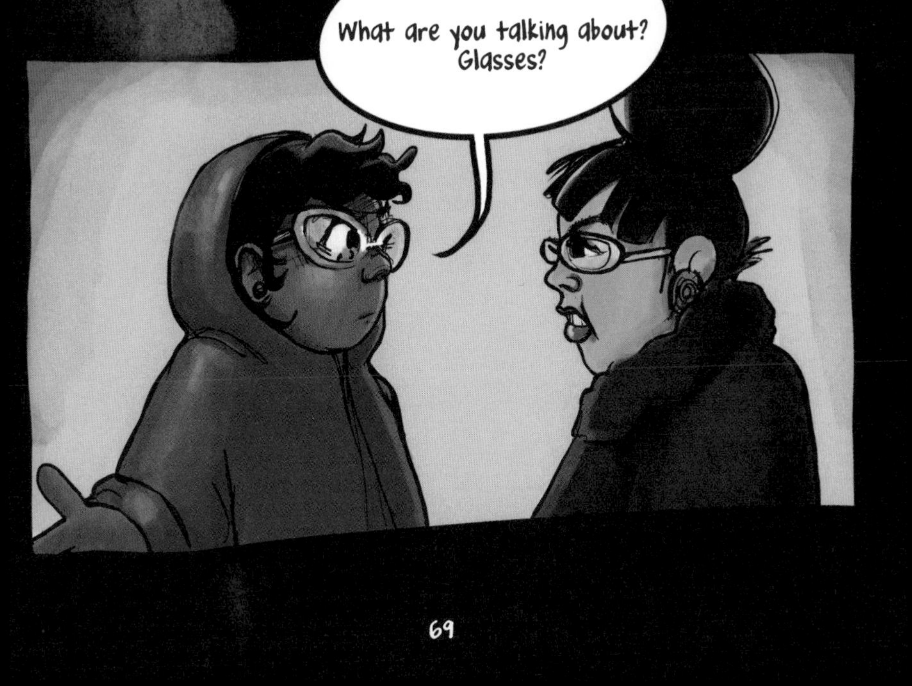
What are you talking about? Glasses?

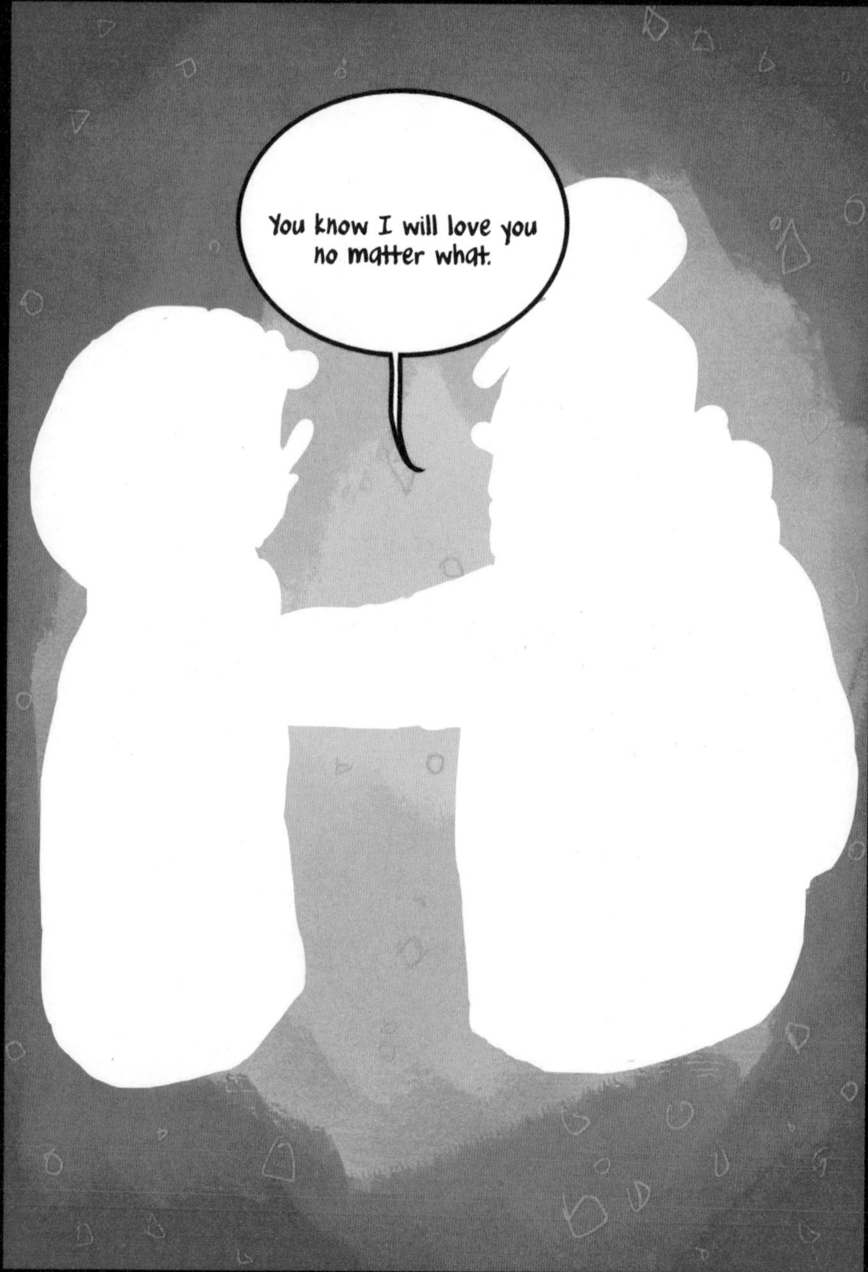
You know I will love you no matter what.

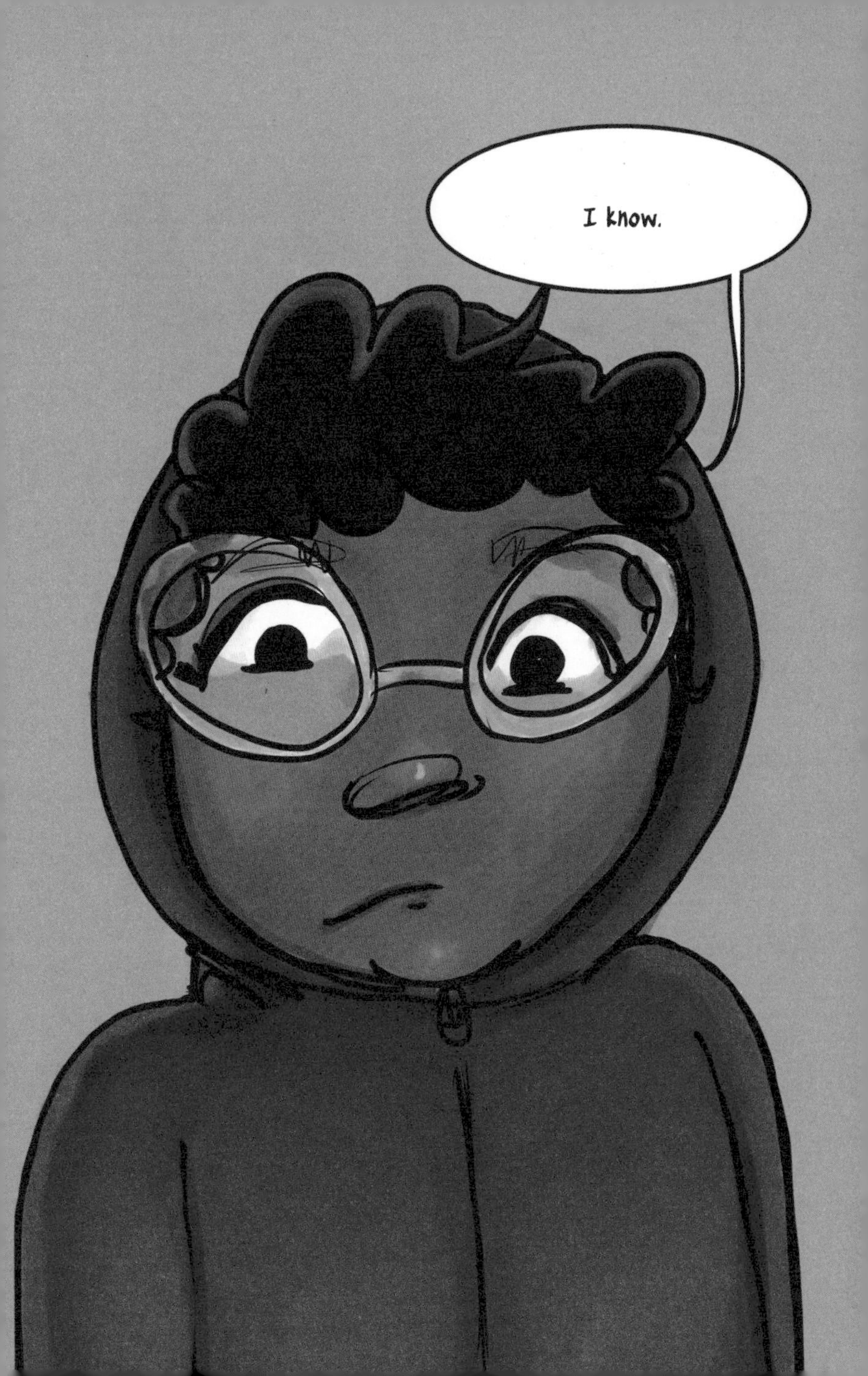
I know.

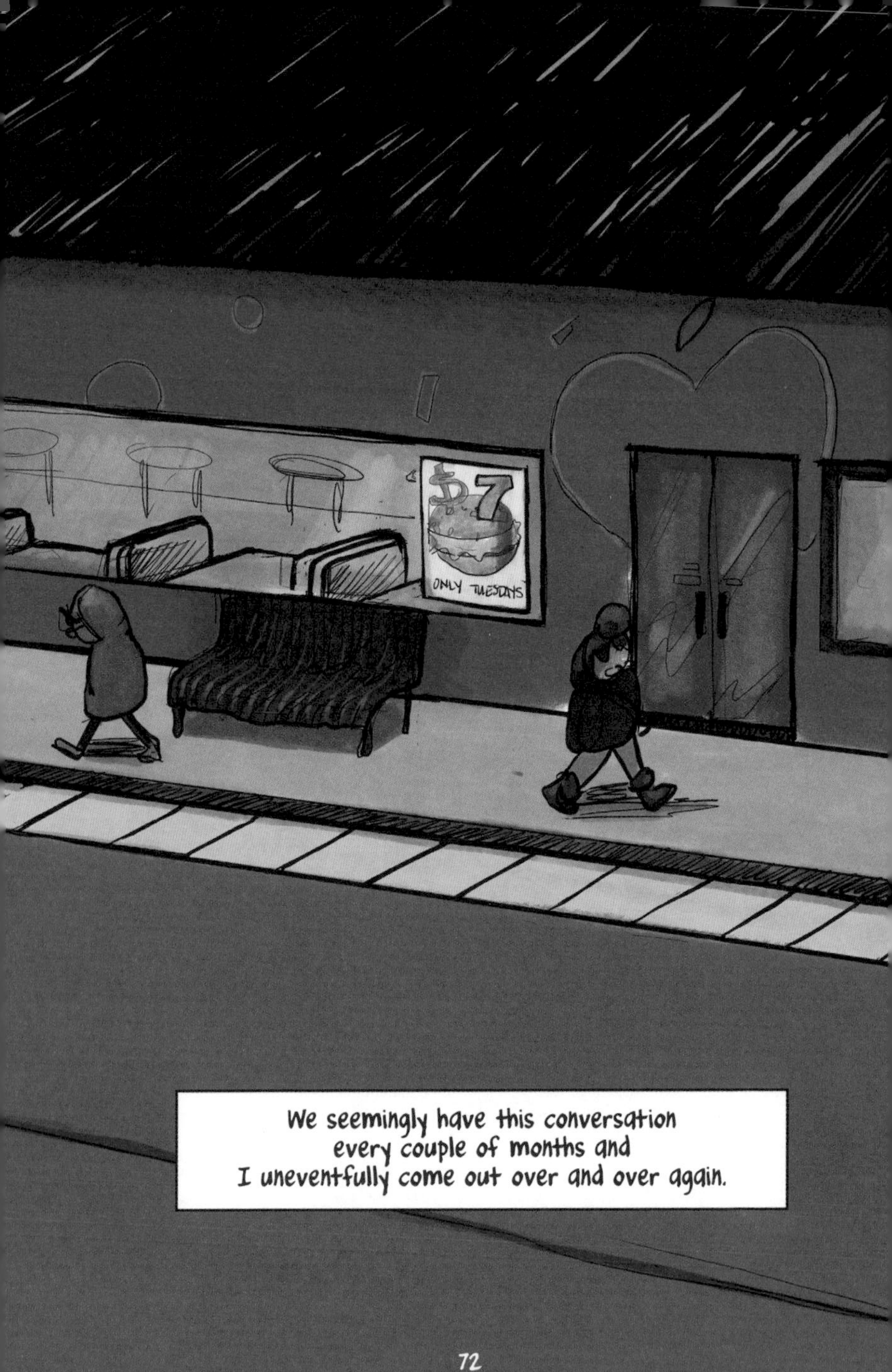
$7
ONLY TUESDAYS
We seemingly have this conversation every couple of months and I uneventfully come out over and over again.

VERY
GAY

Decolonize

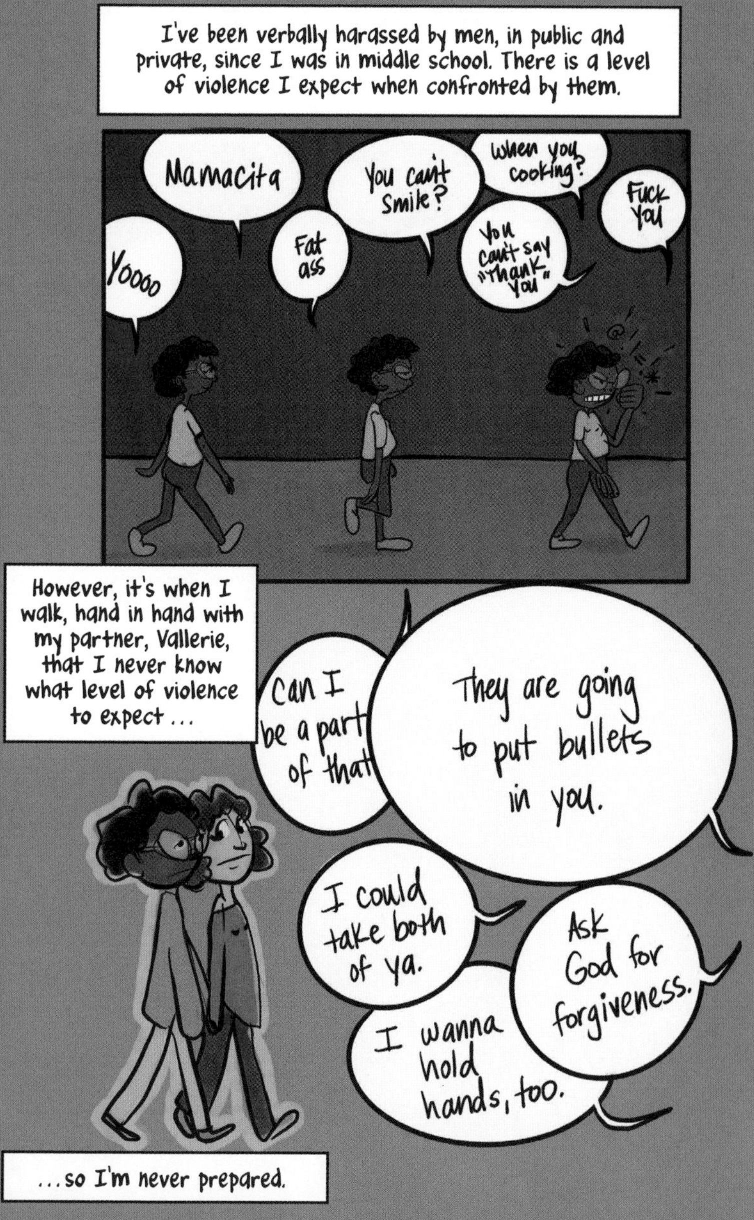
I've been verbally harassed by men, in public and private, since I was in middle school. There is a level of violence I expect when confronted by them.
Yoooo
Mamacita
Fat ass
You can't smile?
When you cooking?
You can't say "thank you"
Fuck you
However, it's when I walk, hand in hand with my partner, Vallerie, that I never know what level of violence to expect . . .
Can I be a part of that
They are going to put bullets in you.
I could take both of ya.
Ask God for forgiveness.
I wanna hold hands, too.
. . . so I'm never prepared.

This harassment accumulates in your spirit, and although I understand where the ignorance and violence stem from, it doesn't mean that those words are not impactful. It's traumatic and, frankly, sometimes I feel like I need to escape.

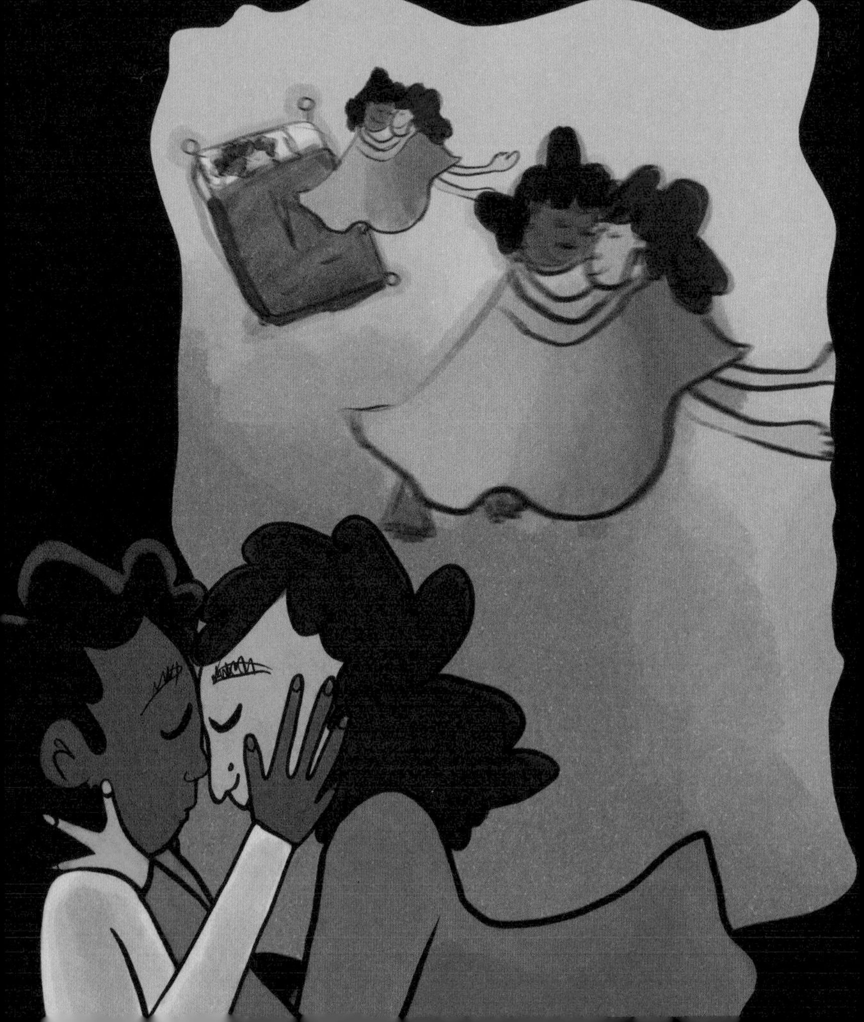

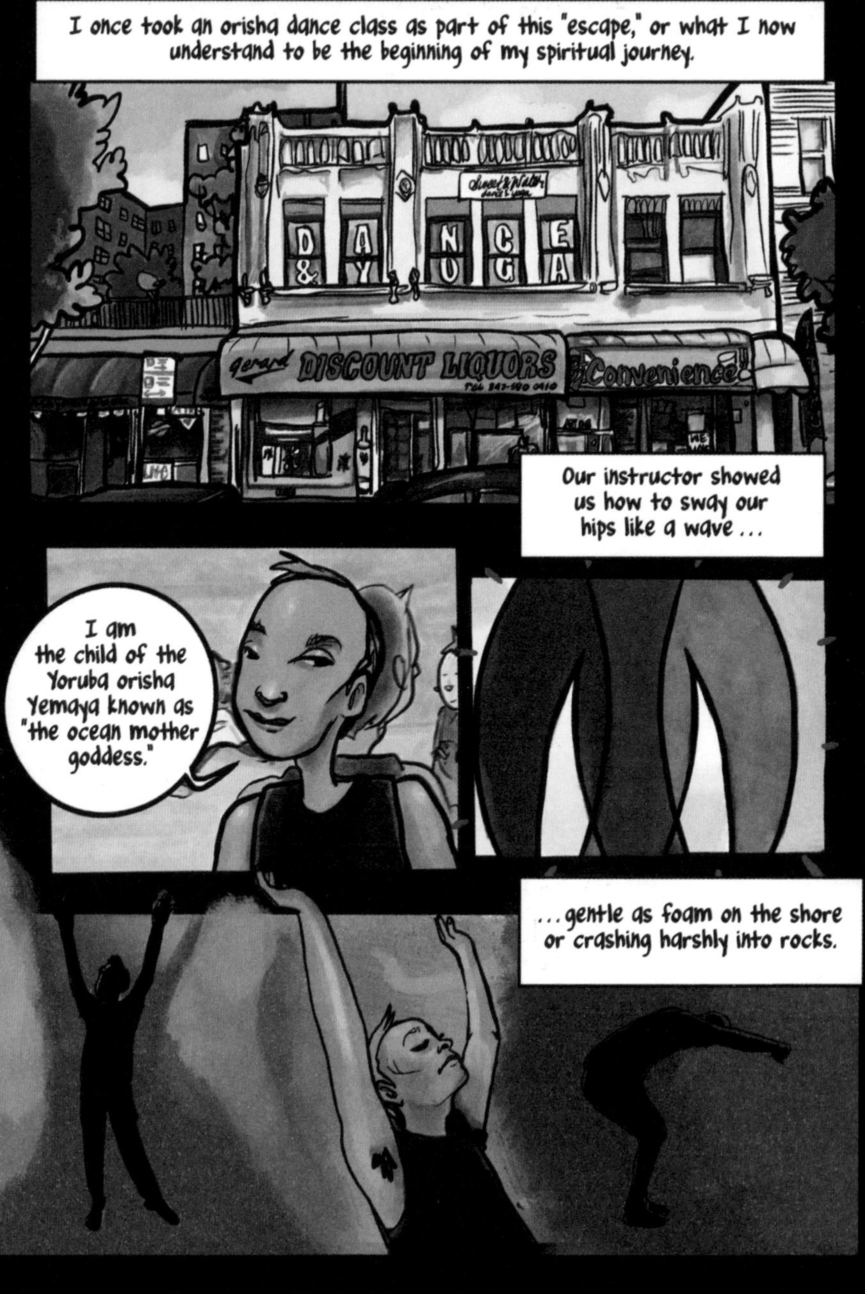
I once took an orisha dance class as part of this "escape," or what I now understand to be the beginning of my spiritual journey.
DANCE & YOGA
DISCOUNT LIQUORS
Convenience
Our instructor showed us how to sway our hips like a wave . . .
I am the child of the Yoruba orisha Yemaya known as "the ocean mother goddess."
. . . gentle as foam on the shore or crashing harshly into rocks.

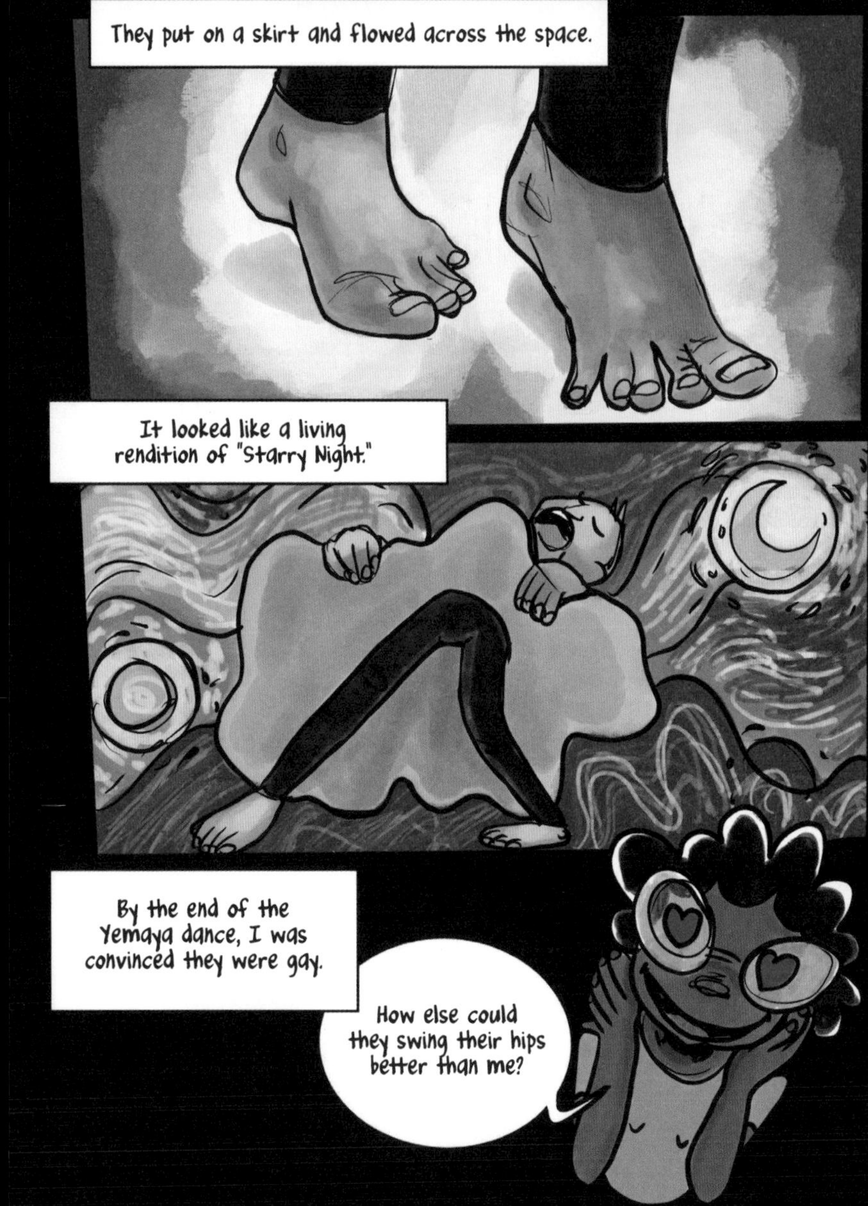
They put on a skirt and flowed across the space.
It looked like a living rendition of "Starry Night."
By the end of the Yemaya dance, I was convinced they were gay.
How else could they swing their hips better than me?

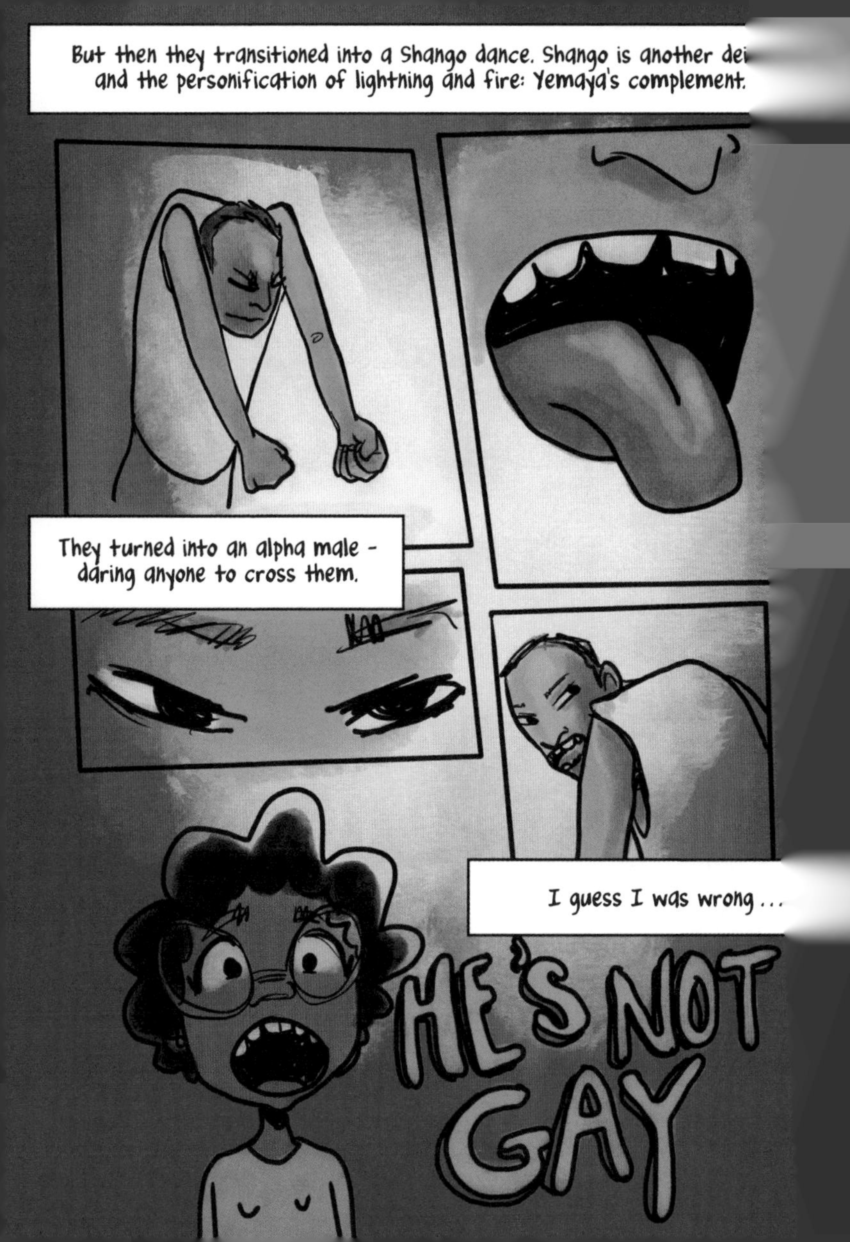
But then they transitioned into a Shango dance. Shango is another dei
and the personification of lightning and fire: Yemaya's complement.
They turned into an alpha male - daring anyone to cross them.
I guess I was wrong ...
HE'S NOT GAY

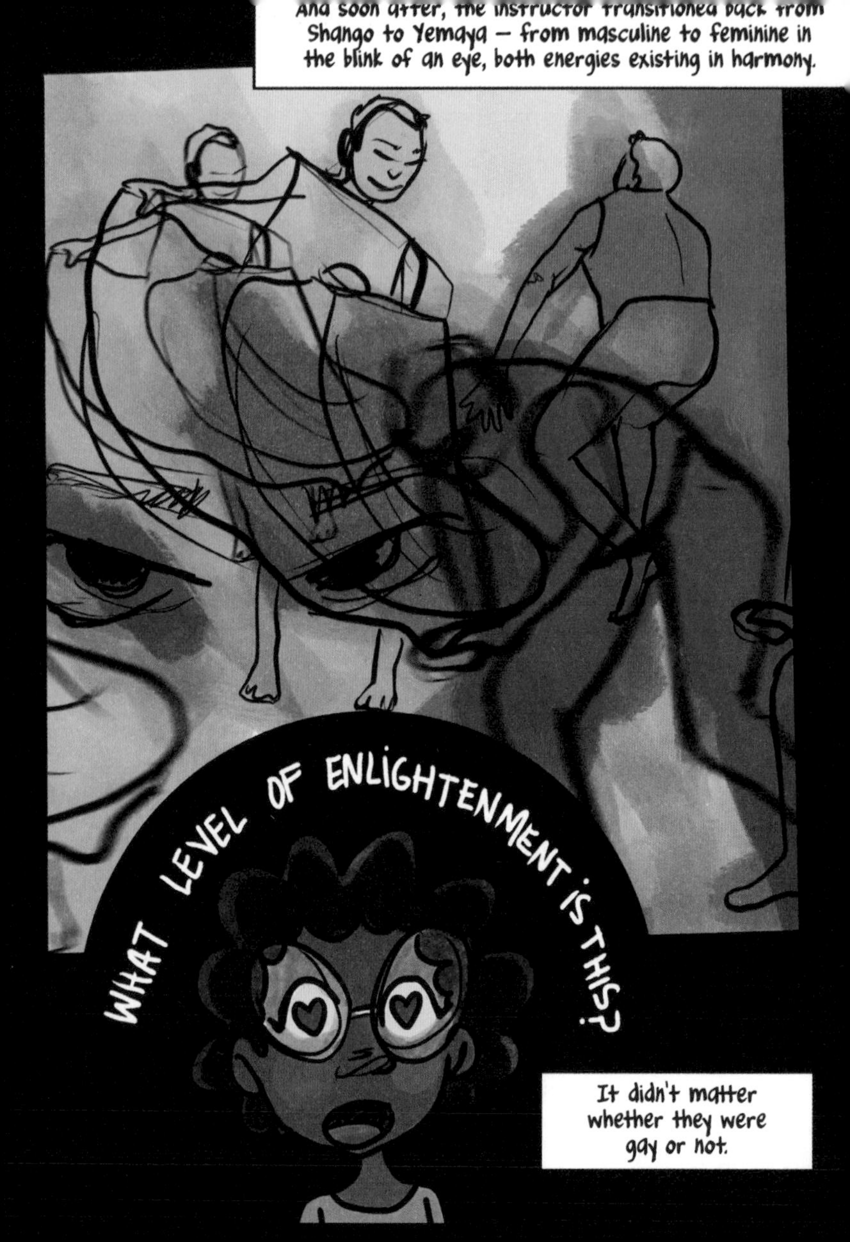
And soon after, the instructor transitioned back from Shango to Yemaya – from masculine to feminine in the blink of an eye, both energies existing in harmony.
WHAT LEVEL OF ENLIGHTENMENT IS THIS?
It didn't matter whether they were gay or not.

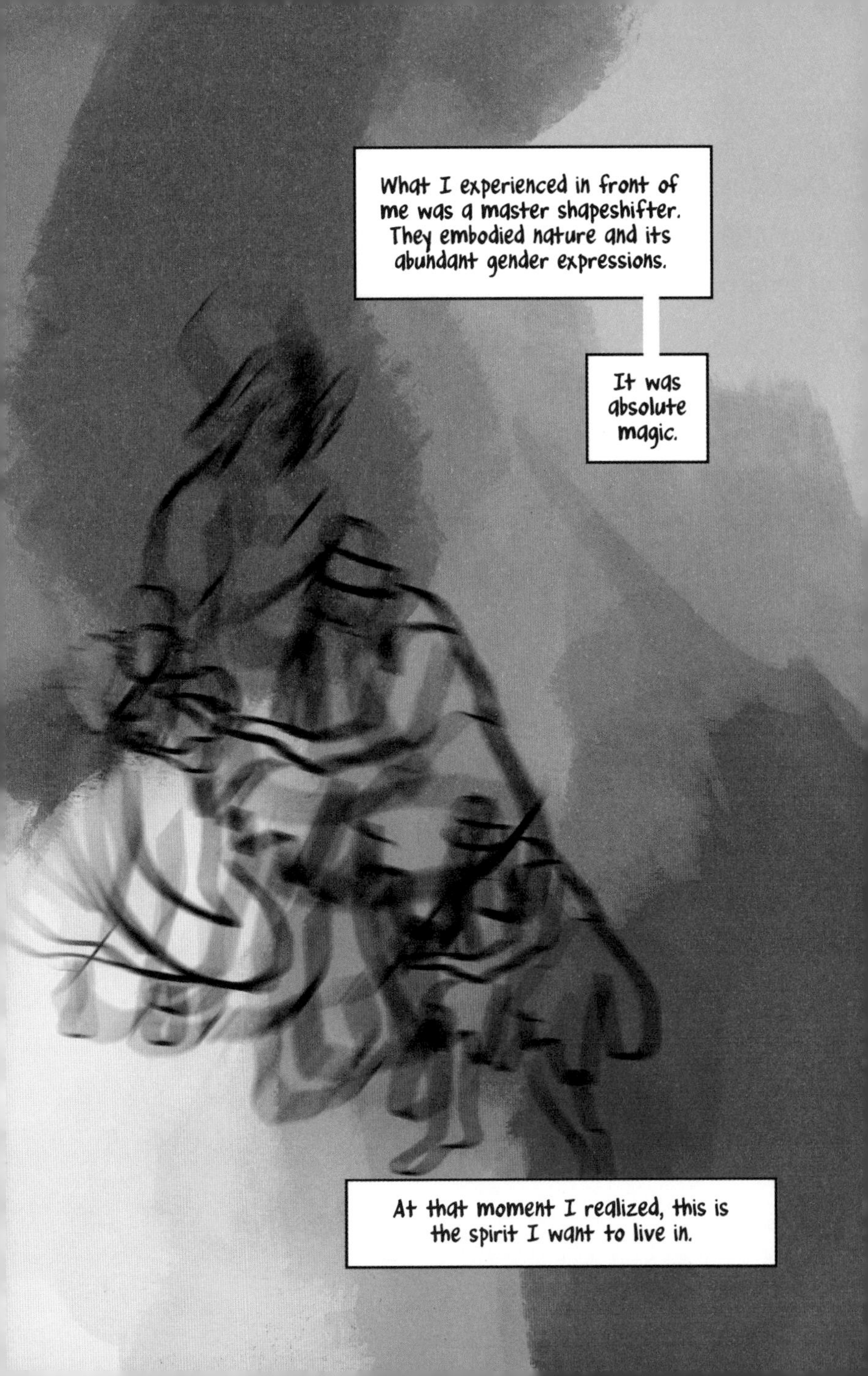
What I experienced in front of me was a master shapeshifter. They embodied nature and its abundant gender expressions.
It was absolute magic.
At that moment I realized, this is the spirit I want to live in.

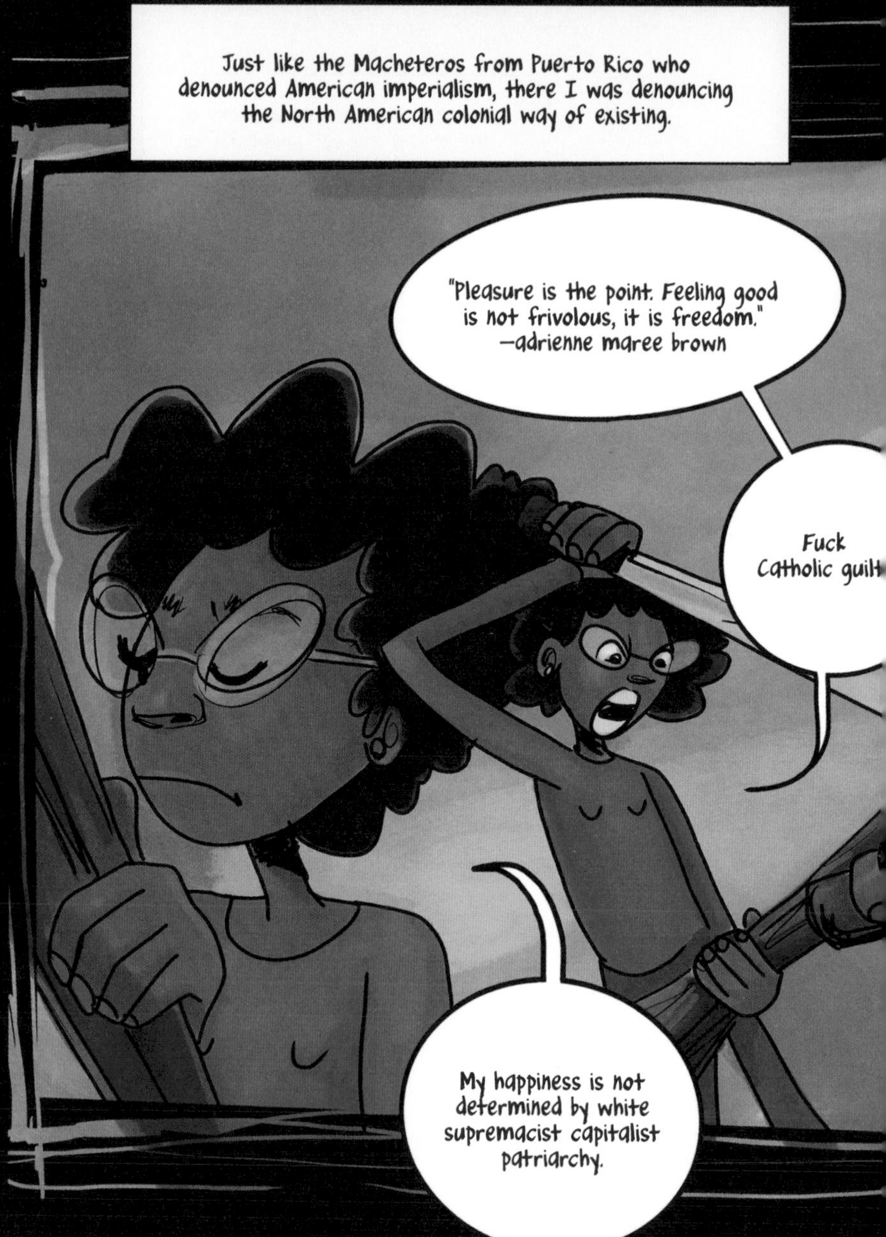

Just like the Macheteros from Puerto Rico who denounced American imperialism, there I was denouncing the North American colonial way of existing.
"Pleasure is the point. Feeling good is not frivolous, it is freedom." —adrienne maree brown
Fuck Catholic guilt
My happiness is not determined by white supremacist capitalist patriarchy.

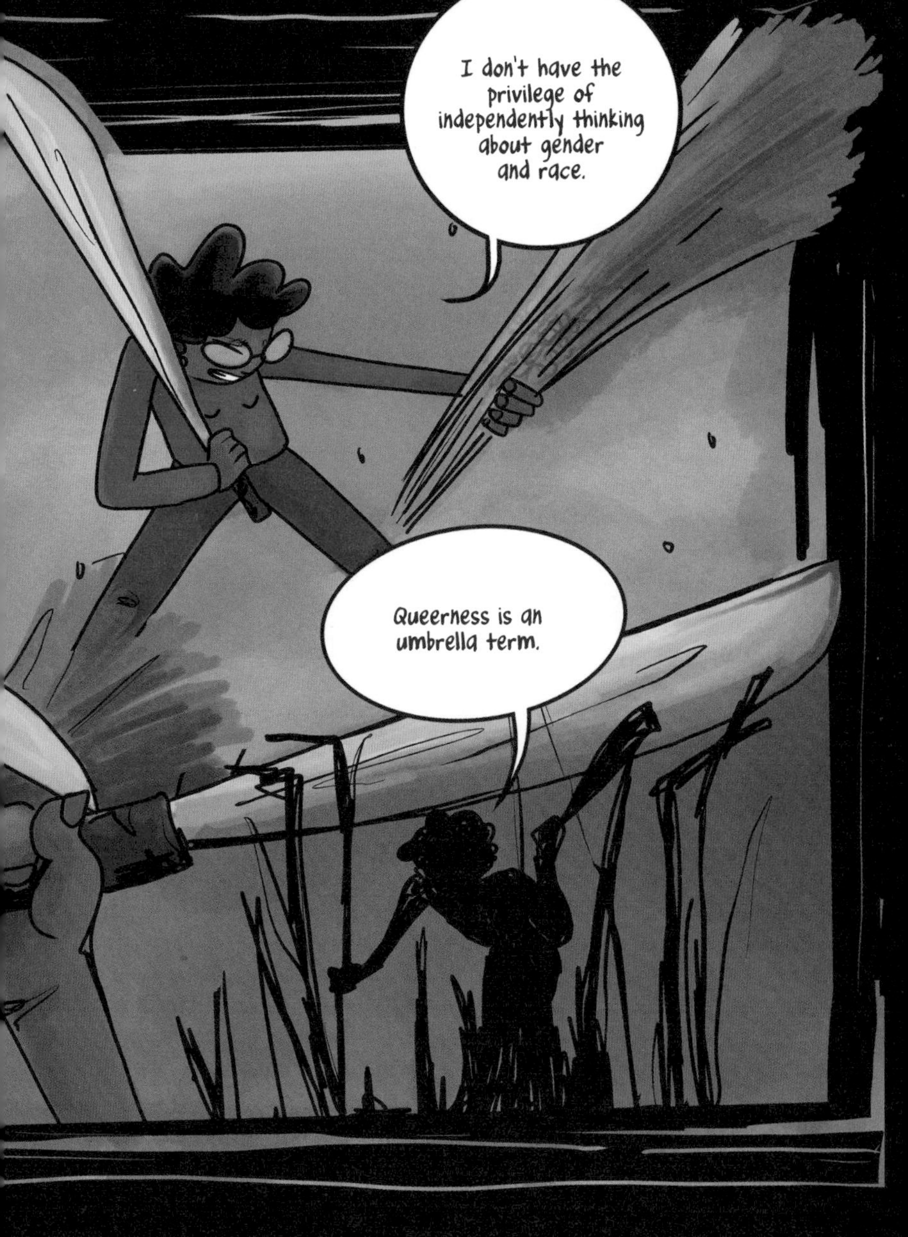
I don't have the privilege of independently thinking about gender and race.
Queerness is an umbrella term.

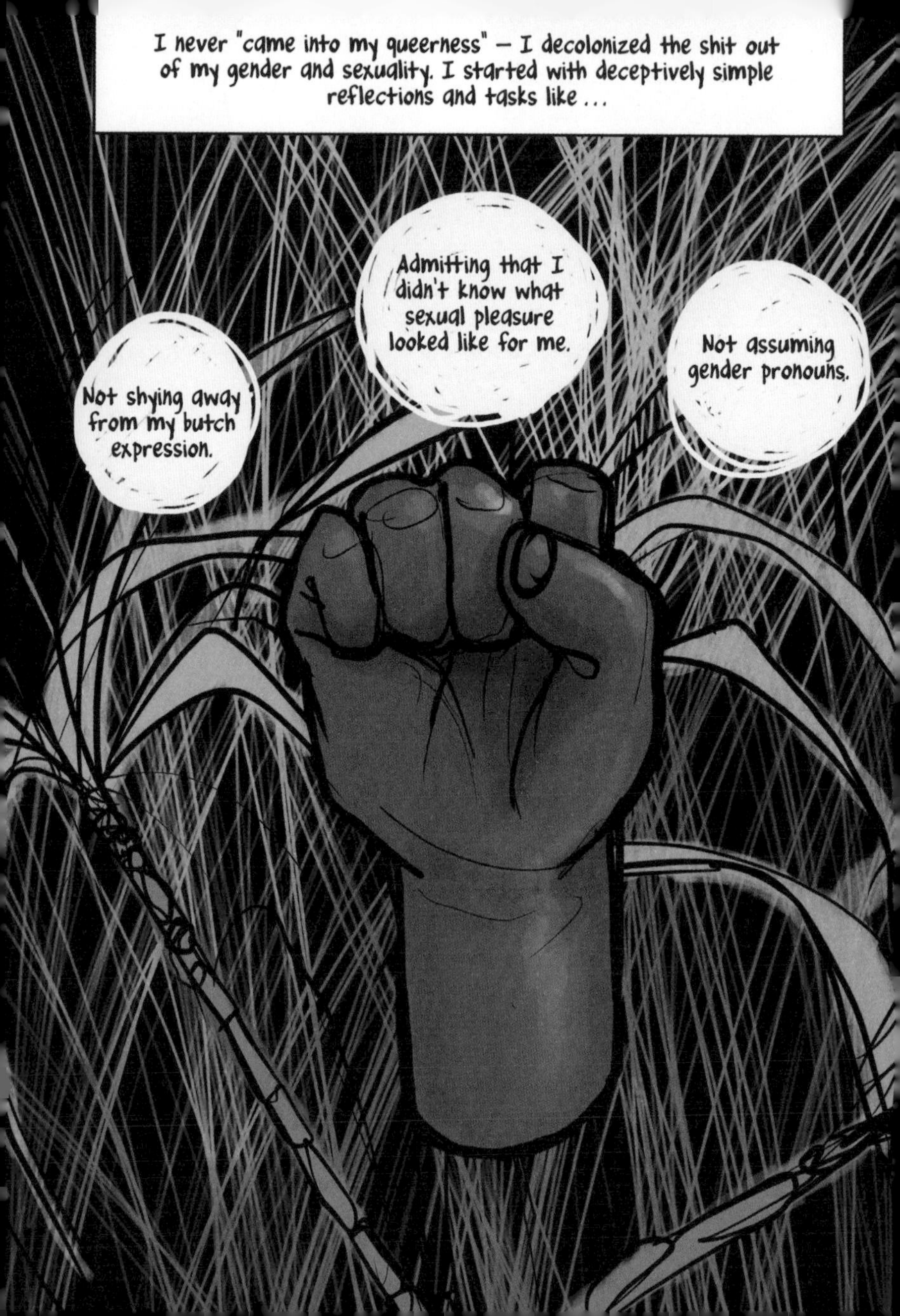
I never "came into my queerness" – I decolonized the shit out of my gender and sexuality. I started with deceptively simple reflections and tasks like ...
Not shying away from my butch expression.
Admitting that I didn't know what sexual pleasure looked like for me.
Not assuming gender pronouns.

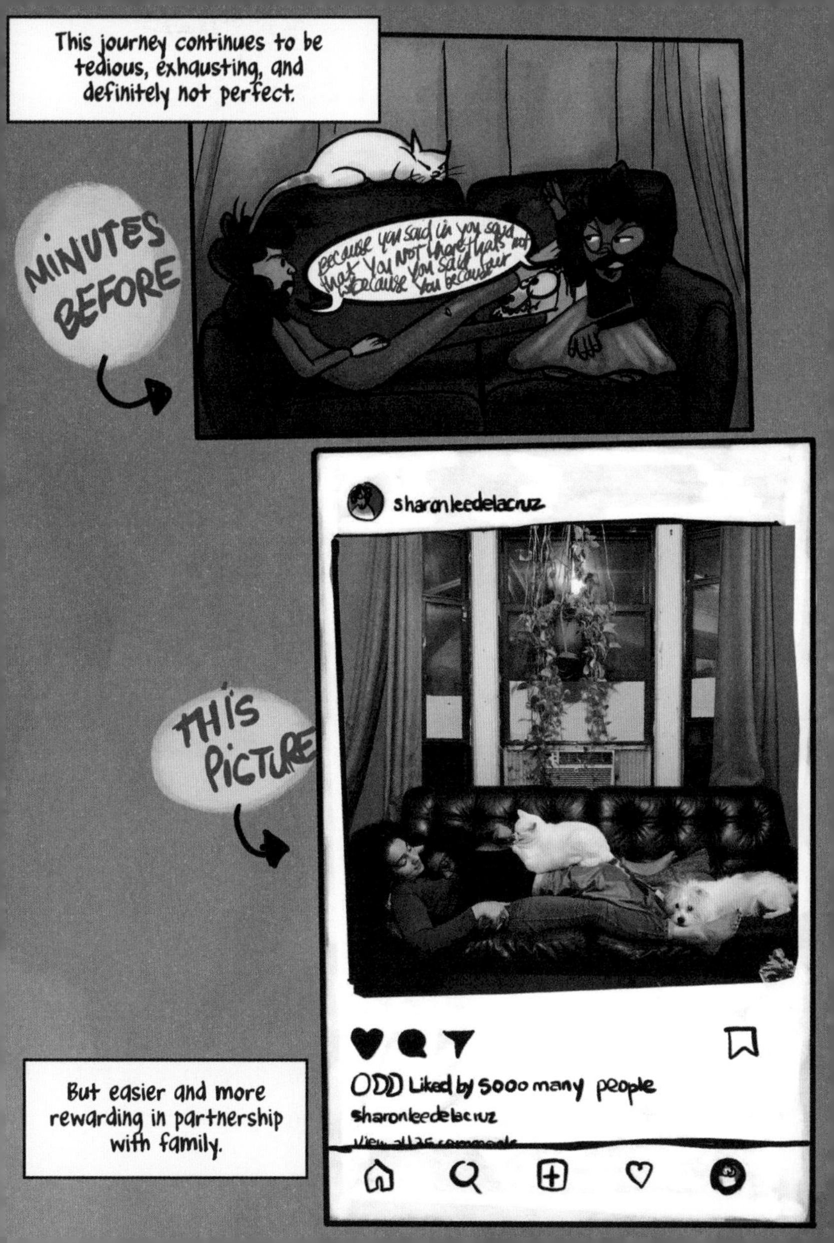
This journey continues to be tedious, exhausting, and definitely not perfect.
MINUTES BEFORE
because you said in you said that you not there thats not fair because you said you because
THIS PICTURE
sharonleedelacruz
ODD Liked by sooo many people
sharonleedelacruz
But easier and more rewarding in partnership with family.

• RESOURCES •

I realize that I touch on some really
complicated concepts in this book,
and I've only scratched the surface.

I, myself, have learned about these things
late in life and I don't think that's fair.
So I decided to sprinkle these gems
all over the book in hopes that you
will be inspired to do your own research.

Here are some things that I found helpful:

• Books •
Zami by Audre Lorde
Anything written by Octavia Butler,
but especially Wild Seed
Pleasure Activism by Adrienne Maree Brown
Sister Citizen by Melissa Harris-Perry
The Altar of My Soul by Marta Moreno-Vega

• Videos •
Dr. Melissa Harris-Perry's speeches on YouTube
The "Stonewall Uprising" episode of American Experience on PBS
The Death and Life of Marsha P. Johnson, a documentary film
on Netflix

•LGBTQIA+ Organizations•

DOOR.ORG (The Door NYC)
THETREVORPROJECT.ORG
SRLP.ORG (The Sylvia Rivera Law Project)
GLAAD.ORG
TRANSLIFELINE.ORG

I've given you the sandbox,
now start digging in...

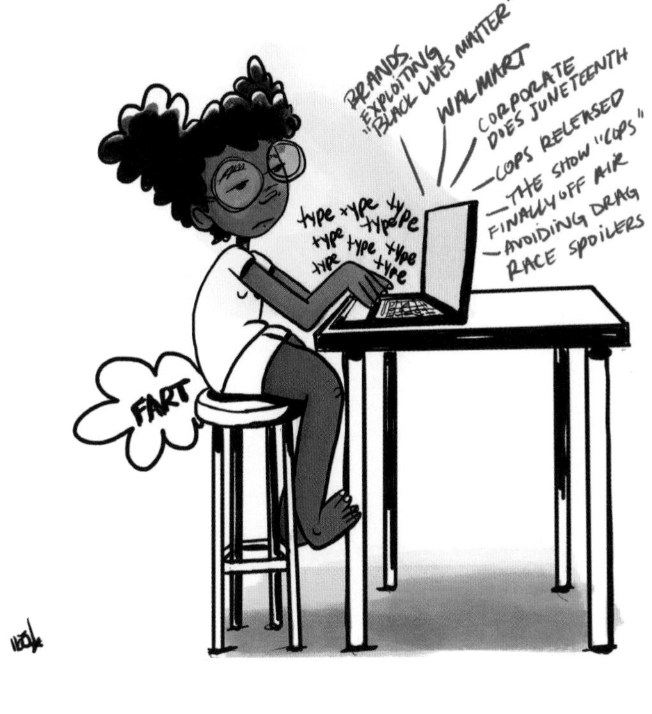
BRANDS EXPLOITING "BLACK LIVES MATTER"
WALMART
CORPORATE DOES JUNETEENTH
—COPS RELEASED
—THE SHOW "COPS" FINALLY OFF AIR
—AVOIDING DRAG RACE SPOILERS
type type type type type type type type type type
FART

• ACKNOWLEDGEMENTS •

I want to thank Word Up Community Bookshop/
Librería Comunitaria for providing a safe space to
present Wild Seed when it was just a tiny zine;
Ellen Lindner for guiding me through storytelling;
Tin House Summer Workshop for pivoting this book
in a way I couldn't do by myself;
my mom for the best/weirdest memories;
and my partner Vallerie for reading through
drafts at 10 p.m.